The Woman
Herself

The Woman Herself

Judith Burnley

HODDER AND STOUGHTON
LONDON SYDNEY AUCKLAND TORONTO

Acknowledgments

Lines from 'Fare Well' reproduced by kind permission of The Literary Trustees of Walter de la Mare and their representative, The Society of Authors.

Lines from 'Marina' reprinted by permission of Faber and Faber Ltd from *Collected Poems 1909–1962* by T. S. Eliot.

Lines from 'Manhattan' by Rodgers and Hart © 1925 E. B. Marks Music Corp, USA. Reproduced by permission of Francis Day and Hunter Ltd, London WC2H 0LD.

Lines from 'Dedicated to the One I Love' by The Mamas and Papas © 1957, 1967 and 1971 Duchess Music Corp, New York. Reproduced by permission of MCA Music Ltd.

Jacket illustration: The Sleeping Woman (1936) by Henry Matisse copyright © S.P.A.D.E.M. 1985.

British Library Cataloguing in Publication Data
Burnley, Judith
   The woman herself.
   I. Title
   823'.914[F]   PR6052.U6574

   ISBN 0 340 38792 0

Hodder and Stoughton Editorial Office: 47 Bedford Square, London WC1B 3DP.

What seas what shores what grey rocks and what islands
What water lapping the bow
And scent of pine and the woodthrush singing through the fog
What images return
O my daughter.

T. S. Eliot from Marina

1

Sarah went from room to room of the old country house, pausing at the doors of half empty bedrooms, standing at odd corner windows, gazing at green and grey and amber coloured mosses on the broken tiles of stable roofs, or clouds moving and light changing on distant hills, or trees and more trees and an expanse of uncut lawn. Rob had left a tape of his favourite Handel pieces running for her – how thoughtful he was – and the stately sounds seemed to fill each room she wandered into with the serenity of eighteenth-century sunlight, though the day was a moody, windy, restless kind of day.

The curious smell of closed rooms in old country houses hung heavily around her and she sniffed it appreciatively. There was something Puritan about it, cold and clean, yet she liked it. The air had a bottled quality, as if the windows had been closed on some bracing morning long ago in another era, but the freshness had remained.

Now, Sarah prowled around, investigating, opening drawers which gave off the clean, sweet smell of ancient wood, finding old sweaters, old photos hidden in cuff boxes, an old black Bible, a phial of little yellow pills, a polyfoto (blurred) of his ex-wife, a ready-made bow tie. Shamelessly, she turned the postcards on the mantelpiece and read the messages of love from other women, scanning snapshots – girls with dogs, with ponies, with new-born calves – for clues. She learned nothing that she had not guessed at, but she made the knowledge hers, wrapping his house, his estate and all its mysteries around her. Should she make these hers, as well?

Rob expected her to do so, she knew. Rob believed that it was only a matter of time before Sarah and her small son David would leave London and their hectic London life and settle here, in Cornwall. All these empty rooms and uncut lawns, unweeded flowerbeds, the shrubs and hedges wildly overgrown, the paddock and the woodland with its tangled undergrowth, the stream, could all be hers. He was offering her so much. And wherever she went in all this spaciousness, George Frederick Handel's measured tones followed her every tread. At the end of the fifth repeat, Sarah began to find his patience a trifle insistent. We live, after all, in more impatient times. She located the old-fashioned repeating eight-track cartridge player in Rob's upstairs study, went in, and switched the music off.

At once a silence so complete, so tangible, descended, her own heart beat too loudly in it. Holding her breath, she pushed the hair back from her ears and listened to it: it was the silence of a house that has been lived in, loved in, and is waiting, with that solid insistence that Handel's music and old houses have in common, to come alive again. She stood still and let her breath come easily as she felt the place settle comfortably around her. How long it was since she had been alone, how seldom in her busy life did she have time to explore the relationship between herself and the space around her. Now, she could feel the old bones of this old house settle shelteringly around her, just as the hills and woods and rivers outside, and all the secret places in the countryside, enclosed and protected the old house.

As she descended the stairs, the wooden treads creaked, each in its own crotchety voice. In the kitchen the clock ticked, the kettle hissed on the Aga, and Guinness, the enormous wolfhound, whose coat was the colour of the froth on Ireland's favourite stout, snored in his basket by the stove, smelling of dog. In the long drawing room, the applewood logs Rob had put on the fire when he and the others had left for the pub crackled and popped and sent out spurts of green juice and sparks which fizzled before settling into ash that smelled sweet on the slightly damp air. She'd have two hours, at least, she reckoned, alone, by herself, to feel at home in his house. Perhaps she'd surprise them all by cooking lunch for them, and having it ready for when they returned, full of beer and whisky chasers, hoary old jokes and anecdotes of the local eccentrics they'd encountered.

She sank into an armchair and listened to the flames of the fire as the wind fanned them hard against the chimney breast, and the loud purr of the cat in front of it, and became aware that it was not silence that enveloped her like an old blanket, it was solitude, the calming quiet of the country one heard so much about, a quiet full of noises of its own: the creaks and groans of the old house, the fire, the swaying of branches in the wind, the moan of the wind itself; it was sudden, cold interludes of birdsong, the scurry of small wild animals through grass, the pad of domestic animals on wooden floors, or their thin, urgent scratching at doors to be let in, or out. Even the beat of her own pulse, or the swish of her needlecord jeans as one thigh brushed the other when she moved. Was there no such thing as silence? Certainly not here, in the country, where everything breathed, snored or purred as rhythmically as the seasons.

She picked up a book Rob wanted her to read and gazed thoughtfully at the title – *Household Ghosts*. In that special way he had of knowing things, Rob had known that Sarah must be left alone in the house to settle down, in spite of everything that had happened, for there was no fearful, final silence here, only a deep healing peace. It seemed the Celtic peoples knew about grieving, and about healing, too. And Sarah was much too familiar with the first, and not familiar enough, God knew, with the second.

She read a few pages of the book – it was difficult stuff – but she could not concentrate. Well, that was nothing new. Since Adam's death she had found it impossible to concentrate on anything except the tape that went round and round and round in her head: the dreadful jerks his poor body had made from side to side, left right left, after his heart had stopped; the colour draining from his face; his profile settling into awful stillness; and the tear, that solitary tear which travelled the delicate track from eye, along nose and across the curve of his cheek before it fell. One tear in lamentation of a life! If only she could stop it, stop the tape and never see any of it again. Never. Never. Never. Never. Never.

Yet she knew it wouldn't stop. Seven months and seven and a half days later, she was no nearer believing in what had happened. She had seen it with her own eyes. She had been forced to watch her husband die.

And that, as she was fond of saying, was something else, a whole extra experience. It isn't given to many. Not just death. Not simply, or only, or merely the Big D, but having to look it in the eye.

Sarah had known Adam since she was sixteen and three quarters and he eighteen. She'd loved and resented, indulged and placated, laughed at and encouraged him every day since then. Yet in the end, neither the intensity nor the habit of that caring had had the power to save his life. And now, when she made her Delphic utterances about the difference between experiencing a death and watching someone die, people recoiled, as if flinching from an essential truth which she, Sarah, had been forced to face and understand.

How could they know that she could not approach the meaning of her own oracular words any more than they could, though she knew that she spoke the truth? Sarah understood only that the dreadful tape would not stop playing in her head until the moment she believed what she had seen. And there was no way she could believe in the fact that Adam was dead, let alone accept it.

His presence was so strong in her that when she dreamed about him, the vividness of his special smell and feel, the familiar clothes he wore, the funny lop-sided way he held his right shoulder when he walked, held no surprise for her, and she awoke calm and relieved. He was there. He was with her. They were together. The dream had simply proved that they would always be together. And when she contemplated the dream during waking hours, which she did with pleasure, she thought only: I shall never be truly "with" anyone, ever again, so completely was I on his side.

11

It was that "new person – us" against the world. It can never be otherwise. Ever.

With a startling sibilance, a log fell off the fire and was caught, fiercely flaming, by the fireguard. The cat watched her in supercilious silence as she struggled, scarlet-faced, with tongs and poker, and eventually got it back into the fire.

She went into the kitchen and prepared the roast, deriving great pleasure in culling herbs for it from just outside the kitchen door. A leg of local pork! With what pride they'd bought it – or she'd bought it – when Rob had chosen it. She'd better not put it on just yet. He'd never forgive her if it were overdone – nor yet if it were underdone, either. Perfection was barely tolerated in this house. She remembered with amusement and exasperation what Rob had said on another occasion:

"Next time you roast pork for me, Mrs. C., see that you rub salt on the crackling!"

She prepared the vegetables – Rob was very fussy about them, too, and would doubtless have done them better himself. He was always lecturing her on the dangers of foreign food. "The skin may be delicious," he'd say, "but these Cyprus potatoes aren't grown in good clean earth, as we grow them here. For all we know they're raised in filthy foreign dung. It's not enough to scrub them. Look here – you've left an eye," and he'd grab the peeler from her and gouge it out. She laid the table and then she and the immensely aristocratic wolfhound, who clearly felt Sarah to be an inadequate swap for his master, went for a walk around the grounds.

Thoughtfully, Rob's ex-wife had left macs and wellies in the outhouse in Sarah's size, but she couldn't find Guinness's lead. This meant that she had to keep up with him in case he got through the cross-barred gate and chased the neighbours' sheep, and Guinness's energy after his long snooze by the Aga was prodigious. After an exhausting half an hour, Sarah took him back to the house, shut him in the passage with his basket and his Sunday lunch, went down to the cellar for more logs for the fire, banged her head on a beam coming up, took an apple and a chocolate biscuit and went out again, alone.

Above the house and across the drive on the edge of a steep little wood was a swing, tied to the high branches of an elm. Sarah sat on the swing and munched her apple and swung, gently and then more bravely, watching the roof of the house and the chimneys and the smoke from the fire she'd just stoked rise and fall against their backdrop of trees and the hills beyond. And she thought, Here I am, swinging above this house which could be mine, this perfect country house nestling in the valley, in harmony with the trees and the curves and slopes around it, in scale with human life. I'm all alone in the midst of deep countryside, not a soul about, and I've been alone for, let's see, three and a half, nearly four hours, and yesterday I was in London and next week I'll be in Paris and where's Adam?

You see, she said to him, swinging up and down, high and low, you see, there's my dream house at my feet, the one I've always said I wanted. You could never see the point of it, could you? You had no feeling for the countryside. Not enough cinemas about, you always said. Well, there it is. And it's waiting. Waiting for me. Inside, there's a dog in a basket, a cat by the fire, and the Sunday roast all prepared. And then a moment of pure eeriness came over her: was it real, this house, this way of life, this country solitude, so suddenly and curiously hers? The whole place seemed suspended in time, as she on the swing was suspended above it. Rob and the others had vanished. What if they never came back? Am I being fanciful, absurd? I've been asked to believe that you will never come back, and what could be more absurd than that? Perhaps no one will ever return from anywhere and I will be left all alone in this beautiful house in this still, enchanted valley, for ever.

She clenched her eyelids, held her face up to the sky and abandoned her body to the movement of the swing. Drops of rain fell on her closed eyelids. She blinked and opened her eyes: the house was still there, still waiting. She jumped off the swing and went towards it. Rain. If only Adam's mother, Adela, hadn't said to her once: "Do you think it rains on *them*?" Every time it rained now Sarah thought of them all, turning their faces to the rain. And what was left of a face, she wondered, after seven months and seven and a half days underground?

She shook herself fiercely as she closed the front door behind her and raindrops fell from her hair as she'd seen them do from Guinness's frothy fleece. She made herself a coffee and went and sat by the fire. Should Rob have left me alone for quite so long? she wondered. On my wedding anniversary of all days. She could hardly blame Rob on those grounds, however, as she probably hadn't mentioned the anniversary. There were many small poignancies she liked to hug to herself these days, so fearful was she of attracting extra pity. She was bad enough at coping with the ordinary pity she had to expect every day. What on earth could be happening in the pub, or series of pubs, of such consuming interest? Didn't all watering holes shut at two o'clock on Sundays? They must have gone back to someone's house to continue drinking. Couldn't Rob have driven back to fetch her so that she could share in some of the fun?

Sarah grimaced wryly to herself. Fun! Apart from his voice and his charm and that particular brand of boyish good looks she found irresistible, she'd fallen in love with Rob because he'd seemed so much fun. Who else would arrive on her doorstep at midnight brandishing a brace of pheasants? Who else would drive her to remote country inns whose dark brown interiors hadn't changed in a century or so and proceed to delight the regulars by reciting the local ballads with them, word for word? Last night in the pub she'd been privy to a discussion of the first reference to salmon fishing in literature (Martial after A.D. 43); had learned the source of Fluellen's comments on the subject in Shakespeare's *Henry V* (Aelian's *Natural History*, c.200); and had been introduced to someone known as The Chief Dowser.

Rob was a naturalist, passionately and knowledgeably concerned with the history and the flora and fauna of his native region, so that Sarah – The Townie, as he called her mockingly – might find herself wrapped in oilskins on a sodden riverbank in darkness observing the solemn rituals of Night Fishing, or pulled to a sudden standstill in a bramble hedge to watch the hover of a hawk, or breathing the dim blue scented haze within a bluebell copse.

Life had been full of unexpected castles since she'd

met Rob, of hidden coves, of deep green whirlpools and shallow, pebbly brooks full of fat brown trout. "I'll catch a trout and smoke it just for you," he'd promised, over their very first lunch. He'd kept his word. She still remembered the unusual, fresh texture and mild, smoky flavour of that fish. And she'd never forget the look on his face the first time he'd watched David running in long grass.

"I've always said this place needs children in it," he'd said. "I'm fed up with wasting all my paternal feelings on Guinness, here." He patted the silky fur. "Last time I had a party he stood on his hind legs so he could dance with me." Rob gave a half embarrassed chuckle. "It's time he learned to be a dog again."

So Sarah had discovered a most surprising fact: these unexpected glimpses of the natural world, revealed to her by Rob, possessed special healing powers. The fragility of things: birds on the wing, the delicate tracery of a feather – their very fleetingness – lightened, somehow, her heavy, earthbound grief. Before they'd gone indoors, last evening, he'd taken her to the edge of the paddock where the woods began and shone his torch into the branches of a tree. Two baby owls gazed down at them, coming into focus in the black, surrounding night like little, feathered revelations. Rob talked to them in owlish, and the baby owls replied, as if to an old friend. "Aren't they lovely?" he said to Sarah, pulling her close, his voice all pleased and warm and furry at the edges. "There's something to take back with you to London Town!" He moved the light away and they watched a hedgehog, spiky as a chestnut, trundle away into the safety of long grass.

That very morning he'd gathered a blue bowlful of

speckled brown eggs for breakfast, and a saucepan of field mushrooms wet with dew. In front of her place he'd put a tiny pot of daisies. "The day's eye," he reminded her. None of these treasures could have so enchanted her if they had been expected, yet here she was blaming Rob for being unpredictable. As well rely on Rob as on April weather: mere moments of radiant sky made every day worthwhile.

Sarah put the meat in the Aga, and made a note of the time, then she got her notebooks and started work on her interviews for Paris. She was doing a magazine series on Divorce in several countries and had lined up a number of people living in France who were willing to talk about their experiences. She read through the files her researchers had made on her interviews and began to annotate them. When the others returned to the house she had been alone for seven hours.

It was evening and growing dark outside. The birds' twilight chorus was dying down and the guilty noises, whispers and giggles, and the sounds of uncoordinated limbs banging into things seemed magnified. They crept in as if they were kids, getting home after curfew, anxious not to wake their mum, and for some reason she could not explain, this attitude fanned an anger so fierce in Sarah that she was almost on the point of tears. She was not their mum, nor their keeper. Why should she care what time they came home? Or if they came home at all? She ignored them busily, keeping her head down to her notes. When she looked up, Rob was looming over her.

"Hello, Missus Scribbler," he said brightly, off-key. She managed a tight little smile.

The Lamberts came into the room looking seedy,

their usual yellow complexions almost green. Joan sat by the fire and confided to Sarah in a mournful tone: "I'm not supposed to drink." Then added, under her breath, "I was never used to so much in one day . . ." Her husband grinned liplessly, like a skull. "No food," Joan Lambert continued in her sepulchral monotone. "They didn't seem focussed on food. And I had to drive them back." Her husband left for the loo in a hurry.

Rob hovered nervously about, glancing at Sarah and trying out apologetic looks followed by boyish grins. For the first time since she had met him, six months ago, Sarah did not find those boyish grins disarming: Rob, too, looked unappealing, his skin pale, his cheeks unshaven, his eyes red.

"You'll find your roast pork on the Aga," she said. "Cold. I took it out when it was done."

"Are you *very* angry?" he asked, sympathetically, trying a compromise.

Sarah stood up without looking at him, her notebooks clutched to her chest. "I'm not angry at all," she said crossly. "Why should I be angry?" She left the room and went upstairs.

She shut the door of her bedroom behind her and breathed in the cool, damp air, then went to the window seat and sat with her pad in her lap, staring out at darkness. To her horror she found that she was shaking. Startled by something out there in the darkness, a giant crow flew up out of a tree, flapping his dramatic serrated wings, and as he did so a bank of clouds moved away from the moon, and the outline of the hills was lit with a silver rim. Sarah breathed deeply, mindlessly, as she had taught herself to do against the familiar knot of tears that gathered in her throat, and gazed at the shadows changing on the distant hills in moonlight. Some things are permanent.

After a while, she heard Rob's step on the stair. He was whistling and calling out, "Where are you, Missus?" She said nothing, but he opened the door.

"Please," she said, shakily, "please. Don't let's play this scene. It's not the right one."

"Isn't it?"

"I read *Household Ghosts*," she told him. "You and your 'obligatory scene'. Obligatory scenes are for books, not life."

He came to where Sarah sat on the window seat, then slowly and coyly began to strip off in front of her: the buckle of his belt, his shoes, jeans, shirt – and little Y-front pants. Then he held his cock tenderly in his hand and pointed it in her direction.

"I'm going to bed," he said. "I need a kip." He tweaked his cock affectionately. "You could come with me?" he said.

She turned her head towards the darkness beyond the window and when she turned it back again Rob was stretched out provocatively on the bed like a centrefold, hand still on his cock, now half erect.

"Come here!" he commanded. "We'll have those clothes off you."

"No, you won't," she said firmly, "it's much too cold." But she went to the bedside and stared down at him. His body was sweet, somehow, without clothes. The body of a boy, rather than a man. An innocent-seeming body, despite everything he'd done to it and with it: the kind of body you expected to smell of warm grass. Was that why it always moved her? She lay down beside him, fully dressed, and put her head on his chest, then sat up for a moment and pulled her boots off so she could put her cold, stockinged feet on his burning calves. He was giving out waves of heat like a furnace. A furnace run on alcohol. His breath was so strong she'd probably get drunk from sniffing it, but he stroked her hair, and within minutes was fast asleep.

Sarah lay uncomfortably against him for some time, avoiding the fumes of his breath, wondering whether to laugh or cry, doing a bit of both. If she tried to get up would it waken him? She stirred, but he awoke: in seconds he had stripped her expertly and was fucking her decisively.

"There!" he said. "There!" with that triumphant look on his face. "That's what I feel about you! You can't be angry with me now, can you? Not after that."

If only Sarah had allowed herself to cry, so that the awful tightness in her chest could dissolve in warmth and wetness. Instead, she gave vent to a torrent of words, and the words scalded them both, as no tears could.

"So you, too, for all your Celtic sensibility believe in the oldest myth of all: one good fuck will cure any woman of anything, from vaginal soreness to terminal despair. And to think that I can't even believe any longer in Love as the great panacea for all ills, as I used to do. I know now there are things even Love can't do, never mind fucking. It can't glue the bits of broken lives together. It can't save people from sudden death. Oh, yes, I could have your baby, as you sometimes want me to. I might even be pregnant with it right now. And if I am, it'll be me who has to take all the responsibility all the time. Where will you be? In the pub?"

20

He listened to her as if he were stunned.

"Well," he said. "Well. You've said a lot." And his voice held a serious hurt she had not heard before. Then he turned his whole body away from her, and fell asleep again.

2

Sarah never went straight home from a station or air-port anymore. Nowadays she always went to Mel's house in South London to collect her son David. How lucky she was to have a best friend who ran a nursery school in her own home where David was always quite happy to stay.

Now, the two women sat amid the chaos of Mel's kitchen, drinking mugs of tea. David sat quietly on Sarah's lap in the way he did only when she'd been away from him for two or three days. The heaviness and warmth of his solid nine-year-old limbs gave her an intense pleasure and she rested her chin, then her cheek, dreamily on the top of his head, feeling the texture of his hair, smelling its special odour. This head which had emerged into the world from between her thighs.

Mel looked searchingly at Sarah and raised an eye-brow. "Idyll not idyllic?"

Sarah made a face. "They're in short supply. Even in Cornwall."

"Ah, there be dragons," agreed Mel, and David said sleepily, "I knew there were dragons in Cornwall."

"Oh, you who know everything," said Mel, fondly.

"And thereby hangs a tale. Or tail," said Sarah. "I shan't spare you the details."

Mel nodded, and they sat silently for a few minutes in the ease of each other's company, complete as any family around a kitchen table.

Then a door banged and there were footsteps, and the large, bearded figure of Chris Hemming arrived in the kitchen and broke the mood.

He stood leaning against the wall, surveying them. He had wanted the whole domestic scene, Chris had said, when he had come to live with Mel. He had fallen, not just for Mel, or the nursery school, but for all the warmth and reassuring messiness of the lunatic living style which went with them. He, himself, had grown up a solitary child and had never known family life; he felt it would be wonderful to come home and fall over a tricycle or two before reaching the haven of armchair and double Scotch.

Mel seemed not to notice that he was there. And yet his hairy presence in the kitchen somehow disrupted the harmony that was. Sarah turned to him, uneasily. Shouldn't Mel have given him a cup of tea, or at least said Hello, or even Hi? After all this time, Sarah still failed to understand that Mel was quite simply not man oriented. If Chris had been Sarah's man she would have leapt up and made a fuss of him. Given priority to his needs. Made him the focus of her attention. Mel did none of these things. It had never occurred to Mel to do anything special in order to win, or keep, a man. She simply sat where she was and expected Chris to accept her as she was.

Such confidence made Sarah squirm with envy, for she knew that Mel loved Chris in her way, and liked him, too, yet he was not essential to her, as she and David were, or the children of the nursery school, or the sheltering walls of the house surrounding her. Mel's life did not revolve around a man: her father had been killed in World War Two, and so she had never been witness to that tender ritual, the evening welcome home, the house ready, lamps glowing, pots simmering, everything waiting for that breathless moment: the Breadwinner's Return. Every day of her young life, Sarah had helped her mother in the sacred preparations, watched the slightly nervous smile of anticipation (mustn't look too pleased to see him in front of the child, mustn't look too pleased to see him, anyway). Was that the sound of his key in his lock?

Now, Sarah got up, setting David gently down, fetching his coat, his toys.

"We have to go," she said to Mel. It was a warning. Could any man accept such conspicuous lack of attention for very long?

Coming home was never really coming home anymore. Since Adam's death Sarah had learned to dread the moment she put the key in the lock and opened herself again to the pangs of hope that assaulted her every time. They had agreed, she and David, without ever having discussed the matter, that there would be no pictures of Adam displayed around the place for the time being, but his presence was so strong inside the flat that it was hard to believe that he himself was not, would not, be there. David, too, reacted strongly to this moment. Once, he had come in, stood still and sniffed the air, then run away and hid; another time he had burst into tears just as the front door closed behind them.

Perhaps all the wellwishers, who believed Sarah should move house, had a point. But she did not want

24

to move. They had been so happy here, and besides, she loved the place. It seemed impossible that she would miss Adam less in strange surroundings. Surely she would simply wonder what on earth she was doing there?

And so everything was just the same as it had always been. Except. And the familiar objects, the furniture of their lives, which stood and looked at her, lacked all power of welcome. Even the old armchairs had lost their comfort. But still she did not dare to change a thing. Months ago there had been a leak in the kitchen pipes, but Sarah had resisted the chance to redecorate. How would she know what colours to choose without an argument? Besides, he mightn't like it.

Any moment now, the door would burst open and there he'd be, large and soft and lightly tanned from some trip to the far ends of the earth, distributing hugs and presents and smelling of nights spent in the pressurised cabin of a plane.

David went into the sitting room and switched the television on. Sarah went into the kitchen and put the kettle on. It was all a ghastly mistake, she knew it. Well, it must be, mustn't it?

Just as the kettle boiled, the phone began to ring.

"Pythagoras Price," announced a male voice, pompously. "Or would you rather have Socrates O'Shea?"

"Neither," said Sarah, but the voice ran confidently on.

The inventor of these two preposterous pseudonyms was the obligatory mad psychiatrist met at a party, but

25

because the party Sarah had met him at was the last party she and Adam had attended together only a week or so before Adam's death, Pythagoras Price had elected himself a most unwelcome Chorus to the tragedy and was constantly telephoning Sarah, to explain her own state of mind to her in the latest psychiatric clichés.

With a confidence which betrayed the crass rather than the secure personality, Pythagoras had backed Sarah into a corner at the party and rattled manically on at her about his own neuroses. They were so much more exciting than any his patients came up with, he assured her, even though his patients were a pretty distinguished bunch of the Higher Demented. Right now, he told her, he was juggling with five women, all desperately in love with him; he had to confess it was a bit of a strain even for someone of his libido, as none of them knew about the others. And then there was his wife. He was having some trouble, to his surprise it seemed, in getting an amicable divorce. For a moment his gaze focussed outward and he noticed Sarah.

"Which one is your husband?" he demanded.

Sarah pointed at Adam, across the crowded room. Her heart contracted painfully when she thought of how he was in his last few days. The air of confidence he'd acquired in the last decade had vanished without trace, and he looked as he'd looked when he was very young: desperate, and almost unbearably vulnerable.

In those days he had been afraid that he would not make it, as ambitious young men who've heard about Fate and studied the capriciousness of the gods are apt to be. Now, he was mortally afraid in a way he had never thought to be, for he had always taken health and strength for granted. Now it was his physical, not his spiritual life in danger, for his heart had begun to beat extremely fast and he'd been taken into intensive care, but they could not determine the cause for his heart's behaviour, and so had slowly reduced the rate with drugs and then discharged him. Bewilderment rather than fear showed in his face and uncertainty in his bearing and the awful thing was that she had not seen it. Neither Sarah, nor Adam himself had known he was in mortal danger. And what could they have done, she wondered, over and over in the reaches of the night, if they had known?

The man who called himself Socrates or Pythagoras had followed Sarah's pointing finger at the party and got a glimpse of Adam's face. For a moment he stood quite still and stared, then he turned and looked keenly at Sarah. He seemed disturbed.

"He is very vulnerable, your husband."

And Sarah's heart had thudded then, as it thudded now.

"How are you?" the voice on the telephone boomed. Adela's standard reply echoed in Sarah's head: *How should I be?* But Pythagoras Price wasn't waiting to hear how she was.

"I'm coming round to cheer you up," he announced.

"No, you're not," said Sarah.

"Aha. So that's how it is. You won't be cheered up!" With the air of a conjurer in an old-fashioned music hall, he produced a rabbit from his hat: "Guilt!" It was an accusation made with all the gravity of a diagnosis. "Grief is very largely a matter of guilt," the oracle added, for good measure.

"Not with me, it's not," said Sarah.

27

Oh, the effrontery of it! It takes a highly qualified, even eminent psychiatrist to utter such banality. Even your amateur, your friendly neighbourhood kitchen shrink, would come up with something more interesting or more useful.

"I'm coming round to give you a good fuck."

Sarah laughed. "I see you've succeeded where poor old Sigmund failed. You, and you alone, have discovered what 'a woman' wants."

She cut him off, and went to run David's bath. Then she made them both a light supper, put David to bed and ran a hot bath for herself. From under the bubbles she rang Adela, who reported two demons sitting in a tree.

"They're devils," she said, "and I wish they'd come and get me. There were demons like them in Poland when I was a girl. They're disguised as great black crows, but they're devils all right. They're sent to collect the souls of the people close to people who have recently died. I pleaded with them," Adela said. "I begged them: Oh, please take my soul, and give Sarah back my son. What use is my life? I am old, and he's much too young to die. Take me instead, I beg you."

"Shut up, shut up, shut up," said Sarah, unkindly. If there was one thing she could not stand it was the sound of the old woman weeping. She lay under the vanishing bubbles feeling horribly mean. Why should she stop the old lady's tears because she couldn't afford to shed any more of her own?

And then there was Dolly, Sarah's mother, who could not get used to living alone after a lifetime of marriage. Dolly had been widowed a year before Sarah.

28

"It's different for you, dear," she said accusingly. "You're young."

At last, Sarah got into bed and curled up on her side. How long would it be before she could sleep in the middle of this bed, or even on Adam's side, as if it were all her own? She pulled the sheet over her ear, as Adam had always done, but she did it to blot out the silence: there was no snoring or tossing and turning from beside her.

Each night before I
Go to sleep, my baby,
I whisper a little
Prayer for you, my baby,
Because it's
Hard for me, my baby
And
This is dedicated to the one I love.

The phone rang, startling her. Adam had so often rung her at night from the other side of the world, a disembodied voice from another timescale. Would it be so strange if he rang her now from the Other Side? She grabbed the receiver eagerly.

"Do you want the bad news or the bad news first?" asked her secretary. "He" (being the editor of the magazine they worked for) "wants to cancel your series on divorce."

Sarah gasped. "But that's awful. He can't do this. I've done weeks of work. And I'm booked on the Paris plane on Wednesday morning."

"I know."

"What's got into him?"

"I give you one guess. He's getting divorced himself."

"Well, that should make him more interested, not less."

"It hasn't. It's turned him off."

"He'll get over it. He'll have to. Oh, God, all that research. I've got so many good interviews lined up . . . I want to use them. And I need the money. Does the man realise I'm freelance and I have to earn my living? I know, don't tell me – I should have gone on the staff when Adam died. At least I'd have been sure then of supporting David." She shook herself. "Okay, I'll stop wailing now. Look, Candida, we haven't had this conversation. I'd gone to France. You couldn't get hold of me. Okay?"

There was a pause, then Candida said, hesitatingly, "I don't think so, Sarah. Honestly. You'll have to come in and see him. Tell him all the good stuff you've got, and how he'll have to pay you for it, anyway. That'll turn him round."

Sleep. Thank God she'd stopped waking up every morning at four o'clock.

When you're far
Away from me, my baby,
Each night before you
Go to bed, my baby,
Whisper a little
Prayer for me, my baby,
And
The darkest hour is the hour before dawn.

30

For months she'd woken with a start and a sense of dread, just before dawn, then lain in her own warmth knowing something terrible was wrong. Wondering what it was. Awaiting the hard thump in the stomach that came with memory.

Everything was wrong. Nothing would ever be right again.

Sarah was in the office, pasting up the introduction to her series on divorce and waiting for the editor to call her in. She was enjoying herself enormously, grappling with the priorities of words and space. This series was going to be good, the best hard reporting she had ever done. People would read it with relief, and know that, after all, they were not alone, for here was evidence that others had suffered the same torments, the same appalling losses. The most important lesson Sarah had learned in all her years of working on women's magazines was that each isolated reader believes herself to be an unnatural creature, experiencing abnormal surges of hate and fear and lust. It was always a revelation to discover that everyone else was just as mad or bad as oneself.

What comfort work was, Sarah thought, for the concentration it demanded wiped one's mind clean of other problems, and there was a positive end in view. One could solve things on the page, put the right number of words in the right space in the right order, meet deadlines, and three months later, see oneself in print on every bookstall in the country. It was satisfying, work; no wonder men respected it so much and elevated it over their private lives. For in the world of the emotions, one could never be simply or satisfyingly right; one grappled with slippery things called feelings without solving anything, hoping only, as year followed year, to understand.

How people managed without absorbing work to do puzzled Sarah – all those women she talked to who complained, when their marriages broke up, that they hadn't anything meaningful to do. She felt sure that she herself would have become quite deranged, these last few months, had not the axis of her world spun between the twin poles of love and work which kept her balanced so precariously.

"I don't want it, Sarah," the editor said, stubbing out his cigarette in an overflowing ashtray and immediately lighting up another. "It's too tough and nasty. It's not right for now. People read us for escape."

"People want to survive," Sarah said. "*How to Survive Divorce* in eighteen point bold on the cover will pull them in. It's the same with any battle: you can escape the firing line and run away but the chances are you'll be caught and shot as a deserter. Or you can stay and fight and live to see another day. What you can't face, you can't even *hope* to survive."

"Very philosophical," said the editor sarcastically, pushing back his chair and walking to the window, where he stared out at the rooftops of cleaned-up Covent Garden. "I want to kill it. Can't you get that in your head?" But the back he had turned to Sarah lost its defensiveness the moment he'd said the aggressive words and as she watched, the whole of his wiry, energetic body relaxed into a tired, dejected sag. Sarah stared at the set of his shoulders for a moment, thoughtfully, then went and joined him at the window. She had never witnessed him in a vulnerable mood before.

"You're wrong, Keith," she said passionately. "You're wrong about the readers. Try treating them as adults. Once in a while, they love it. Remember my *Encounters with Fast Ladies*? About that unmentionable subject, growing old. Everyone was against it. And look at the response we had." Should she pull the personal punches, now, and tell him that she, more than anyone, knew how desperate the need is, to survive? "Look, divorce is experienced as loss," she began. "As a form of bereavement. People mourn their dead marriages – "

He wheeled round and said, accusingly: "But there's an appalling sense of failure, too. 'Failed marriage', isn't that the phrase? Divorce carries all that – like bloody stigmata – with it. You don't feel you've failed when you're bereaved."

"In a way, you do," Sarah said. "Especially if you are the wife. Or widow, as I must learn to say."

He looked at her then, intently, for the very first time that morning.

"Isn't the love of a good woman supposed to save men from fates worse than death?" she added, in answer to the question in his face.

"I don't understand why on earth you want to handle this material. It must be very painful for you. And yet you're fighting for it." He paced over to his desk to put his cigarette stub out. It was scarcely quarter of an inch, she noted with amusement. He smoked them to the bitter end, still the boy from the poor Glaswegian background.

"On the contrary," said Sarah. "I've found that people in the throes of divorce are often in much worse states than widows. There's the breakdown of ego, the sense of failure you mentioned, the whole horror of practical factors – homes and settlements and legal stuff and money. And none of us can stand rejection."

Their eyes met over this last word of Sarah's, and she noticed, not for the first time, what an intense blue-green his were and how thickly they were framed by dark lashes and eyebrows. Today, however, they lacked their usual sparkle of derision, and Sarah saw that, instead, they were filled with pain.

"I believe in the value of this material," she told him. "And besides, I need the money. I don't get much in benefits, you know."

"I only met your husband, Adam, once. I knew him on the box, of course. But from that one meeting I can imagine something of what his loss must be."

"It takes one strong-willed character to recognise another."

"How long is it now?"

"Eight months on Monday next. At eleven twenty-five p.m. *Eight months!*" She looked at him without seeing him, astonished.

"What are you doing for lunch?" he asked. "I could use a drink."

Keith's club had recently converted one of its panelled cells into a ladies room, a sign of the times, indeed. Sarah darkened her eyelids, added fresh mascara and scent and brushed her hair. Why was she doing this? She

34

didn't want this man. Did she want him to want her, anyway? Or was she using feminine wiles to win her own way at work? All this was a reflex action: one must look one's best, one is lunching with a man. She'd be giving conflicting signals, for a change. She supposed she must be receiving conflicting signals from herself.

When she got to the table she found he had started the champagne and was on to his second glass. "The only tonic," he said, toasting her. Sarah felt the delicious, cold bubbles fizzing on her tongue.

"This is so rash, so ill-advised, so sudden. You've always been horribly tough on me before."

"There you go again. Critical. Argumentative, even over champagne. Impossible. You're just the kind of girl I should have married."

"And that makes being tough on me okay?"

"I married the girl next door. They didn't have girls like you next door, where I came from."

"Is that what went wrong? You've outgrown her, or she hasn't kept up with you? All that stuff?"

"I don't want to talk about it."

"There you are! How can I get the man's point of view, which you say, quite rightly, is missing from the series, if every man I speak to clams up the way you've just done?"

"I'm a good husband. I don't expect you to believe me, but I am. Now if I had someone my equal – Sarah, what's it like, managing on your own?"

The steaks arrived, so they drained the champagne and started on the Nuits St. Georges. Sarah sampled her entrecôte and speared a mushroom before replying.

"Essential," she said.

The famous eyebrows shot up. "What do you

mean?" For a moment, the deep-sea eyes rekindled with curiosity.

"I mean that we are all, essentially, alone. So we have to learn, at some point, to be alone with ourselves. I never had to – neither have you – until now. I see this disaster that's happened to me, the ultimate tragedy, something that never should have happened, as pushing me to do so. To stand up, and learn to be myself. It's funny, but most of us don't do it, until we're pushed."

"No man is an island, entire of itself – "

"People suffer personality breakdown when they're left alone because what they had was a dependency." She looked at him across the table in the velvety dark of the panelled booth. "I believe in love," she said, "not in dependency. And before you can give or receive that kind of love, you have to stand alone. For years I was half of a couple. I don't want to be half, or part of anything, I want to be whole in myself."

"It's very difficult."

She giggled. "If anyone had told us how hard adult life would be, we'd have none of us grown up."

"I thought that was the trouble."

"With you lot, yes."

"You can talk. When you laugh like that, you look about fourteen."

"Well, that's a relief. I've been feeling a hundred years old, just recently."

"Sarah, will you spend time with me? I need – I don't know what I need. Look, here's a number you can reach me at, anytime." He scribbled some figures on a book of matches and handed the booklet to her. "Okay?" He squeezed her hand, then turned it over in his palm and looked at it. "I've always liked your hands."

36

"Funny," she said. "I've always liked *your* hands."

"Never!"

They sat there for quite a while.

"Shall I carry on then, with divorce?" she asked him, as they crossed the road to the office, in the unwelcome glare of afternoon.

He shrugged. "For now. I'll talk to the market research people."

She supposed it was 'yes'.

"Thank you for lunch. I enjoyed it."

"Me, too."

She went into the office loo and the book of matches he'd written his number on fell into the bowl. "Well, there you go," she said, flushing it away. "I doubt if I'd have used it, anyway." Her head ached from all the wine and the tension there'd been between them. She'd get no more work done that afternoon.

3

Fully dressed, except for her shoes, Sarah sat in the middle of a large double bed and stared at the roses sent to welcome her. The roses stared back. Here she was, in Paris, in a low-ceilinged, whitewashed room with thick, uneven walls and heavy dark beams, a vase of pink roses, a fridge fully stocked with everything from Perrier to champagne, a bathroom hardly bigger than the fridge but equipped with luxury bubble bath and spicy-smelling soap. It was the start of a cool summer's evening in June, and here she was in Paris in *tout confort*. Alone.

Outside her window in the narrow little Left Bank street it seemed that the same students of her own student days still milled around, tightly packed into the same blue jeans. On the corner, a stall selling incense sticks and another selling South Sea shells; the Rue de Seine market closing, and the flower sellers wrapping each tight bouquet even tighter, before the watering of the streets. Boys met girls, matches were struck, Gauloises lit up, passions flared. One boy punched another, and a girl ran off, crying, her heels tapping on the cobblestones. It seems there's one fiesta which lasts out everybody's lifetime – the party that's never over in St. Germain des Prés.

Sarah leaned out and the well-remembered scents and sounds rose up at her. Guitars were strummed and tunes hummed, and they were the same tunes. She found she could even remember the words.

> Longtemps, longtemps, longtemps après
> Que les poètes ont disparu
> Leurs chansons
> Courent encore
> Dans les rues . . .

Humming herself, now, she turned from the window. Should she open half a bottle of champagne? Better wait for Rob. Strange there was no message at the desk, no curly head waiting to greet her downstairs in the dark cupboard of a lobby, no boyish figure crammed into its own tight, well-washed jeans, curled up on the bed, asleep.

"I've missed you tree-mendously," he'd said on the telephone last night.

"Good. When are you coming over?"

Wasn't the cheque she had sent him on some other pretext enough to cover the fare?

"I'm not going to tell you my plans. I want to surprise you."

"Well, hurry up. The streets outside are jammed with lean-hipped youths plucking at guitars. I want my own homegrown version. I can't think why."

"You won't get your strings plucked till I get there, will you? We don't want any foreign vibrations interfering with our tune." Rob chuckled softly and she thought that even his laugh was in conflict with itself: half light-hearted appreciation, half unease.

"It's like a perpetual party, here," she'd said. "I'll lean out the window later and see if I'm serenaded."

"Ah, ye of little faith," said Rob. "I'll be there. The airplane timetable's right here in front of me."

> La foule les chante un peu distraite
> En ignorant le nom de l'auteur
> Sans savoir
> Pour qui battait
> Le coeur . . .

The telephone shrilled and she leapt to answer it, but it was not Rob, downstairs, at the airport nor even at the Gare du Nord. It was someone she knew on one of the French women's magazines. It seemed they had managed to get her invited to a party.

What should she wear? She pulled open the heavy old wardrobe door and gazed at the clothes she'd bought yesterday, on impulse, at the boutique next door to the hotel. She had been given a bundle of francs to cover her expenses: "Come on," she'd heard Adam say, "we'll buy you some things with this." She had surveyed the racks of brightly coloured clothes, selecting the ones she thought he'd fancy, replacing those to which she thought his voice said "Ugh!" He, alone, knew how she was supposed to look. Did he not place her at the centre of his world, composing the frame anew each morning, through his viewfinder? Since he had died, Sarah had no idea how she looked, for he was not there to tell her, and the absence of the mirror, which for so long had faithfully reflected her to herself, made her feel invisible.

Why wouldn't the skeleton go to the party? ran one

of David's ridiculous skeleton jokes. Because it had no body to go with.

She had bought a jumble of summery clothes, shaken them all out on to the bed in her room and tried them on in front of the long mirror; but no voice reassured her and she had decided they were all mistakes. Now, she selected a charming skirt and waistcoat trimmed with rick-rack braid, but was uncertain whether to put a plain white blouse with it, or a black cotton tee-shirt. Alone, it seemed that Sarah was uncertain of more or less everything: what she was supposed to look like, why she was here, where she was going. She was so unused to looking at the world through her own eyes, she had never dared to look at herself, at all.

A room full of aggressively modern furniture, and melancholy, old-fashioned people. And noise. Sarah would have preferred the street party, any day. Why had she come? To blot out the dreadful tape, she supposed. To forget the sight of Adam, dying. To be distracted from the thought of death. She felt a desperate need inside her to be reabsorbed into the stream of life.

An elderly couple stood out from the crowd because of the contentment on their faces, so Sarah sought them out, and they turned out to be the parents of one of the three hosts. They had come up from the country, the old man explained, holding the old woman's hand and stroking it. They had wanted to celebrate their anniversary with their boy.

"We've been married forty years," the old man

beamed at Sarah, full of pride. "And every morning I take her up her *café complet*, and every evening she prepares for me a little feast."

"And now we are getting old," confided the old woman, her eyes seeking a friendly chair in vain. Her husband supported her with his arm and continued to stroke her liver-spotted hand, twisting the wide gold band of wedding ring beginning to loosen on her bony finger.

"I don't know what I'd do if she went," he said to Sarah, in tones quite audible to his wife. "It doesn't bear thinking of." He fixed his gaze mistily at the farthest wall. "She'd manage, you know, without me. Women are so much more practical, don't you think? But I'd be lost. I don't know what I'd do."

Oh, God! She'd walked into it again. She'd have to discuss experience of loss and offer advice about how men could manage alone. She couldn't bear it. How could she escape?

Across the room, she saw two women magazine editors she'd interviewed earlier about divorce. Judging from their expressions, they were having a lively discussion over generous tumblers of whisky and soda. Sarah got herself a vermouth and asked if she might join them.

"I'd like to kill the bugger," said the one called Stella, jabbing the air viciously with her cigarette, and referring, it seemed, to her ex-husband. Sarah bit her lip. The woman hadn't said anything half as vivid to the tape recorder. "The worst thing is, after all he did to destroy me, he's out there somewhere walking the streets of Paris with his new wife on his arm and his new child, all dolled up in a pram; he's eating and shitting and fucking – damn it, he's even laughing and having fun. I wish I were dead."

Sarah rummaged in her tiny evening bag for pen and paper: she was some journalist – she didn't even have an eye pencil, let alone a notepad.

"It would have been better," Stella said, "if I'd let him come home from America alone. We lived there for a year. He was working there. That's where the marriage broke up, you see. I could have stayed there with the children and made some kind of different life, but I wanted to come home, to France. I never reckoned I would feel like this about it. Every night he goes home to an apartment full of furniture we chose together but *he* said was his, and pictures I chose which *he* said he liked. Christ, when I think of it! It all comes down to possessions, to prosaic and boring *things*! Do you remember the incident of my *escritoire*, Christine?"

Christine nodded, and took another swig, while Stella rattled on. "He came with the furniture removers and he took almost everything, even things that had been given to me by my mother." She turned her head to Sarah but her eyes were too full of humiliation to focus clearly. "Even now I find it hard to believe he could act like that," she said.

"When a man leaves his wife for another woman," Christine said to Sarah in rapid French, "he deals her the ultimate rejection. She feels destroyed. I do not know why this should be, but it is difficult for her to believe that she was ever loved, ever beautiful, desirable, serene. It is true, *n'est ce pas*? Overnight, a pretty woman becomes a person who has never been worthy of love. A failure."

"One has to begin again," Stella said, in her bitter,

43

edgy voice. She tapped her nails against the glass she held. "From scratch. One has to build a new life in a vacuum, the vacuum *he* has left. One must re-invent oneself, without the comforting furniture of any previous lives." She dragged deeply on her Camel cigarette and looked challengingly into middle distance. "It's hard," she said.

"I was reading an article that said that divorce was much harder for women to cope with than straight-forward widowhood," Christine said.

Stella nodded, and Christine warmed to this theme.

"With divorce you have bereavement," Christine said, "but no proper forms of grief. What makes it harder is the sense of failure, the constant analysis of yourself: that endless picking of the scabs of guilt – the where-did-I-go-wrong?"

"Yes. What did I do? Or not do? Or do wrong?" echoed Stella. "And exactly how was his new woman superior to me. A refined form of torture this." She gave a short, sharp, mirthless laugh. "Was she better than me in bed? Does she have larger tits, or a tighter bum, or soft blonde pubic hair that matches the hair on her head?"

Here it was again. Was there no escape?

"A widow has to face all the grisly facts of death," Sarah offered. "She's supposed to accept the unacceptable."

They rounded on her.

"Does a widow feel abandoned?"

"Does she feel it was all her own fault?"

"Does she have to analyse the broken pieces of herself to find out why it happened?"

These two women were relentless in their fury.

44

Perhaps they *were* the Furies? Sarah had no intention of declaring herself, even to such Authority, although, as usual, she'd brought the whole thing down on her own head.

> "Humpty Dumpty sat on a wall,
> Humpty Dumpty had a great fall.
> All the King's Horses and All the King's Men
> Couldn't put Humpty together again."

Sarah intoned the old rhyme in a slow, meaningful manner, then grinned at her inquisitors and took a reassuring swig of vermouth. Uncomprehendingly, they stared at her. "An English nursery rhyme," she said helplessly. But even the recital of poor Humpty Dumpty's fate wouldn't stop Stella.

"The worst thing with a divorced husband is that he's alive and walking the streets of Paris with fortune and the future on his arm," she went on, remorselessly. "Tomorrow morning I could run into him again, and just seeing him would destroy my hard-won equilibrium."

Seeing him! How many times these last months had Sarah thought she'd seen Adam in the street, or driving a car, the familiar profile flashing by her in an instant, longed for – gone. Only last week she'd caught a glimpse of him at the bank. He was talking to the girl behind the till, and she knew from the back of his neck, from the set of his shoulders and the hair curling into that slender hollow . . . She must get out of here.

Sarah caught sight of an elderly American painter she'd known for years. "Someone I know," she muttered to the two divorcees, and went towards him.

A small, wiry, attractive man, Humphrey G. seemed much more wizened than she remembered. To her surprise he greeted her by kissing her wetly on the mouth, then enveloped her in a fierce hug, and gripping the tops of her arms quite painfully, steered her towards a couple of small, uncomfortable chairs he'd spied, hidden in a corner.

"Sarah," he said, turning a rheumy eye and a powerful blast of ginny fumes upon her, the juniper berry still fragrant and not unpleasant on his breath. "Oh, Sarah, did you know Peggy died last week?"

He caught her hand and held on to it. "You knew she was ill, of course? She wrote to you. The awful thing is – my new exhibition opens tomorrow. I've just finished hanging the paintings. It was all arranged, you see, and I couldn't put it off. She wouldn't let me. She felt sure she would live to see it. You know what an optimist Peggy is – I mean was."

He caught his breath, which fluttered a little in his throat, then jumped up and pulled Sarah to her feet. "Come and see! You can have a private midnight *vernissage*. I've got the gallery keys!" He fished in his pocket and jangled them before her.

"Yes. I want to get out of here," said Sarah. But she had wanted to be alone for a while, and certainly not to hear about another death.

Peggy, thought Sarah, as Humphrey rushed her along the street. A schoolgirl name for one of the sexiest, most adult people she'd known. A woman called Margaret. The story of how Peggy and Humphrey had met and fallen in love on a railway station somewhere in Italy, at the tail-end of the war, had long been part of Sarah's mythology. Their pre-war marriages, commitments, countries, had faded before such vivid new realities: they'd gone to live near Lucca among olive groves. They'd been happy. The last contact Sarah had had with Peggy was when Peggy had sent her an envelope by post from Italy. Inside the envelope was *The Times* obituary of Adam, decorated round the edges with laurel leaves done in bright green poster paint. Sarah could picture Peggy sitting up in bed like a sick child, wearing some appalling frilly garment, painting the leaves in one by one, and weeping a little as she did so. Peggy had loved Adam in the devoted way of people who'd worked with him. And now Peggy, too, was dead.

Humphrey stopped abruptly before an iron gate in the wall of an old house in the *sixième* and unlocked it with a massive iron key. They went through the gate, and across a courtyard, up some stairs, and into a long, bare gallery with north-light windows, parquet floor and that exciting air of *chic* exploding into art you find in France.

"Shut your eyes," Humphrey commanded. "I'm about to switch on the lights. Okay. Open – now!"

The long room was a cave of glowing treasures, each picture lit with spotlights to bring out colour without bouncing off the glistening swirls of paint. It had been carefully done, and was essential to show these pictures: enormous canvases smeared with paint so thick and so delectable she wanted to lick it.

"How do you get it on so thick?" she asked, fascinated, unable to resist touching a particularly luscious curl of glistening olive greens. "With a palette knife? It must be fun to do." She sniffed, happily. She'd always loved the smell of oil paint since the first time her parents had taken her, a gawky fourteen-year-old, to the studios in St. Ives.

Humphrey gave her a quick, affectionate kiss, his lips surprisingly soft and resilient in his tightly drawn face, then he linked her arm in his and took her round. Most of the paintings were abstracted landscapes of the area round Lucca, and his streaks and chunks of paint described the texture of rocks near the Carrara marble mines, the feathery plunge of olive trees as they fell headlong towards the sea, the rapacious Italian sky.

"For an abstract painter you're strongly inspired by the elements of place," Sarah said.

Humphrey squeezed her arm and said she'd got it just about right. "Wait here!" he commanded, indicating a dark corner in which some cushions formed a low sofa against a wall. "There's a bar here, somewhere." He clicked his fingers, remembering. "It better not be locked."

Sarah began to doze off and awoke to a delicious smell of gin and the sound of ice rattling against glass.

"Here's to meeting you so unexpectedly," Humphrey toasted, taking a good swallow and sitting down beside her.

"It's a funny colour, this drink," observed Sarah. "What's in it, other than gin?"

"Angostura bitters. You're drinking a pink gin, sometimes known as gin and bitters. It's what I always drink. Don't you remember?"

"Pink gin!" The name conjured the post-war period, the fifties in New York, Humphrey's hard-drinking past so vividly, Sarah blinked and took a gulp herself. "My God! Strong stuff." They'd been serious drinkers before the war, those one-liner toughies who drew for the *New Yorker*. And going off to the front as official war artists didn't soften them up. Endlessly wise-cracking, so as to appear hard-bitten, they got World War Two down in soft pencil line softly smudged, or, whenever there was time, in a more ambitious pen and ink and wash.

Suddenly, Humphrey unzipped his fly, took Sarah's hand and put it on his cock. Oh God! What on earth was she to do without offending him? After a moment, she gave it a polite squeeze, then unhurriedly withdrew her hand, leaning over as she did so and kissing Humphrey gently on the prominence of his cheekbone.

"I'm sorry," he said sadly. "I must be out of my mind. It's just that, since Peggy died, I've been randy all the time. Please forgive me, Sarah. I meant no offence to you. I don't know what's got into me."

He gazed at Sarah mournfully and Sarah looked at the troublesome muscle which lay, pink and purple and blue – reproachfully – between them. She felt she had never seen a sadder thing than this bereaved member which Peggy had so loved and cosseted and cared for. And brought alive.

"Oh, Humphrey. It's the knowledge of death that's got to you. The finality. That's all. There's nothing wrong. Sex and death are so closely intertwined. You know about all that from being in the war. Copulation after battle. Birth rate soaring. It's basic human instinct I suppose. Replace lost life. Perpetuate the species."

To her surprise Humphrey seemed grateful for this absurd and awkward speech.

"I felt so disloyal to Peggy," he said. "As if my urge was to celebrate."

Gently, he put her hand back on the now quiescent

49

curve of the newly bereaved, and her fingers registered the curious rubbery satin of its skin.

They sat there, quiet and perfectly still, for what seemed to Sarah a long, long time. Around them, impressions of the landscape two people had lived and loved in glowed with radiant certainty. They alone could look forward to an unclouded future.

Humphrey escorted her to the door of her hotel, kissed her hand and vanished. How she could do with someone young and silly to make her laugh, to make her forget all this death and destruction which seemed to be everywhere.

There were no messages at the desk, but she went up in the lift, still hoping. She could hear Rob's voice assuming a ridiculous brogue to tell her the end of a whiskery Irish joke.

"Never ye moind, me dear. Oi've somet'in here that'll put new life in ye."

She began to smile as the lift ascended high into the eaves of the tall old building, but when she came into her room there was no curly head on the pillow. She must fall into sleep again, alone.

She awoke, as she so often did at home, to the sound of the telephone, and as she moved to take the call, she saw that a maid had entered and left her breakfast tray and departed again, unheard. She sniffed, and imagined rather than smelled the delicious aroma of fresh coffee, and her eye took in a croissant, a long crisp roll of new French bread, a small brioche and two tiny pots of jam. How delectable French breakfast was! What bliss! With the deftness of long practice in such manoeuvres, she pulled the tray towards her with one arm, and took up the telephone receiver with the other.

"Oh, Rob," she said. "Good morning, love. You're just in time for breakfast. Shall I pass you a chunk of buttered croissant down the phone? French breakfasts are far too good to eat alone."

Was there something neurotic about her desire to share absolutely everything she liked? Was it strange that a grown-up woman found it hard to accept that she should eat the whole of a croissant alone? It seemed odd, or excessive, at the very least.

The voice at the end was faint, but she caught its strained and anxious tone quite well enough.

"It's the bloody Inland Revenue," he said. "I *was* coming, honest I was. But they've summoned me. I've got the timetable of the planes to Paris open right here, I swear to God I have."

There was little more to say. Sarah put down the phone and poured her coffee, but no fragrant, appetising steam rose up at her from the cup. A middle-aged woman knocked and entered briskly. "Are you just up?" she tutted. "Well, you can't drink that. It must be good and cold by now." She seized the pot and bustled off to fetch some fresh, hot coffee, leaving Sarah to blink at such unexpected service. There had been no hint of reproach in the woman's manner. What was it Blanche Dubois had said at the end of *Streetcar Named Desire*?

"I've always depended on the kindness of strangers."

Fortunately, she thought, as she bathed and dressed and conjured up the domes and spires of the familiar city lying, a magic carpet, at her feet, fortunately, Paris is not haunted, because I discovered Paris as a single girl, alone.

Sarah had first come to Paris as a schoolgirl of seventeen, and explored the city by herself, giving the slip, most of the time, to the student party she had travelled with. She had browsed at the *bouquinistes* by the Seine and gazed at pictures and statues and climbed the towers of Notre Dame; she had become addicted to the sting on her tongue of those lemon water ices sold just inside the gates of the Luxembourg Gardens. She did not remember the need to share anything at all, that very first time: she had hugged every image and sensation of the vast, unrolling panorama to herself.

It was true that, since then, she and Adam had visited Paris together several times, but, somehow, it had not become a ghost town, as so many other special places had become, where she had to contend with a host of insistently clamouring memories. She would enjoy being alone today, before and after the remaining interviews on divorce. She would seek out old haunts – the Orangerie, the Deux Magots; she would not be haunted.

The lift, a three-sided cupboard with thickly carpeted walls and no door, lurched slowly down through the heart of the ancient hotel building, alongside the original stairwell, revealing the descending curve of a graceful wooden staircase, the balustrade disappearing endlessly, vertiginously, downwards into the bowels. Without warning, a wave of passionate anger hit Sarah in the stomach, and rose like nausea inside her. She fell, as if pushed, against the side of the lift, the thick, curly-textured surface of the carpet abrasive against her face, inhaling the dusty, woollen smell of it, feeling sweat, cold as sea spray, on her skin.

You never could tell when they would strike, those Furies: within or without, they were everywhere. The other night they had come to her in her sleep, and shaken her body so violently, she'd woken to find herself flung to the far side of the bed. At the slightest sign of hubris, they were there. How dare she believe, ever again, that things could be all right. She who'd been forced to look Darkness in the eye, to see into the pit, the void. She, poor unwilling initiate, who had stood quaking before the Awful Mysteries while they tore her blindfold off. How dare she begin to relax enough to sleep without terrible dreams, or to wake without that dawning sense of dread? How could she believe that Tuesday would follow Monday, or the seasons take their turn, now that she knew the harvest was never to be reaped at all?

Sarah walked slowly along the familiar Left Bank streets, breathing deeply to regain her calm. The sky that summer was heavy and oppressive, the air clammy, the trees a brooding, jungle green. There seemed no lightness, anywhere. In the Luxembourg, children still got their shiny black patent shoes dusty bowling their hoops on the beaten-earth paths so carefully prescribed for them, but the lemon-water-ice man was gone from the gate, and the chestnut trees had been tailored severely into dark green barriers, which cast square, box-like shadows she did not like at all: a Douanier Rousseau picture full of hidden fears.

She sat down heavily on a bench. Once, these chestnuts had put out the clear green leaves of spring, leaves that had patterned whole days with light and air. No one had warned her that summer could be so gloomy an affair. Of course, she was being punished. "My husband

53

died," she heard her voice repeat in her head as it must have done yesterday, and the day before, and the words conducted a stab of guilt, that rusty old knife twisting in the gut again. The statement was a lie, and the Furies knew it. Adam had not "died": he had not acted in the matter; you could not use the word "died" actively, like that. To do so was to betray everything she knew.

Death was something that had been done to Adam. He had been killed, by Death. He had been felled, a tree in the forest, passive as silence or history.

Even her memories of discovering Paris alone were lies, and the Furies knew that, too. For she had not been alone in spirit. Had Adam not written to her every single day of that first trip she'd made away from him – serious schoolboy letters to his schoolgirl love? Had she not found an envelope each morning, on her hard narrow lycée bed, delivered with more than a frisson of jealousy by the fattest and plainest of her classmates? And she had replied to him, she remembered, not every day, but a couple of letters, at least, longing, even then, to share it all.

"Even the white wrought-iron chairs in the parks are in pairs," she had written, "turned towards one another. Conversation pieces among the leaves. *Paris, city of lovers.* Even the bridges have niches just big enough for two."

He met her off the overnight boat train at Victoria. Shyly, he kissed the tip of her shiny nose. "You don't look tired, or awful, as you said you would." He lifted her case and squared his shoulders, manfully. "You look lovely," he said.

She shrugged. He'd been planning to say that, whatever she looked like. She knew.

I "lost" my husband, she thought now, sitting shivering on a park bench in clammy air, so many summers later. As if he had been mislaid. But he's the one who lost. He *lost his life*. No more croissants and coffee for him. No more trips to Montmartre in the early morning mist, no cognacs and Gauloises at the Dôme or the Rotonde, no more garlicky snails Chez Lipp, the melted butter shiny on his small-boy mouth. No more.

She went back to the hotel and rang Mel. "If David isn't missing me, I'm going down south to Italy for a few days. I've had Paris," she said.

4

She took a taxi, she took an airport bus, she paced the airport, she sat in the boarding lounge, she climbed the steps to the plane. So much movement, she thought, so much restlessness. Since Adam died I've been travelling almost as much as he did, trying to emulate him, perhaps, to keep his lifestyle – our lifestyle – going. Trying to escape from the facts: that home was not home anymore; that major change was bound to bring a lot of minor changes in its wake, but what were they to be? And so she went on hoping that maybe, just maybe, there was some place left unhaunted on the earth, and yet unchanged: a place where she could relax.

Tania met her, dressed in a brand-new blue Ferrari and a cool, white muslin djellabah, the voluminous folds of which made her seem smaller, more elfin, than ever. She was bronzed, of course, and the laugh lines which crinkled her eyes were hidden by enormous sunglasses. Her sandals were barely held on to her slim, brown feet by a single brown suede thong and there were no bumps or lumps at all on her toes. She smelled nostalgically of Ambre Solaire. Sarah felt hot and restricted in her neat linen suit and high heels, which had been so suitable in Paris, but Tania's bear-hug, and delighted, throaty giggle had not changed since the day they'd first met at the convent school at eight (Tania said seven) years old.

Sarah sank into the low, seductively upholstered seat and returned the giggle.

"I see that you're wearing this term's gymslip and plimsolls with the same jaunty, stylish air as ever," she grinned.

Tania chuckled and turned the ignition key. The powerful engine purred under her tiny hand – a leopard in captivity.

"And I'm still a crack shot with a plimsoll," she said. "If the nuns are out walking today, I'll demonstrate. Quick, what's the Pope's telephone number?"

"Oh for one Nun."

"And his registration?"

"VAT 69. If you go on like this, I'll *sing*," threatened Sarah.

"There's no choir to go flat."

"There are tyres on this swanky wagon, then, aren't there?"

"Relax," Tania said, lighting a small cigar, "I haven't told anyone, lately, exactly how long we've known each other."

"In the name of the Holy Smoke, I should hope you haven't," said Sarah feelingly.

She caught glimpses of dark, solid buildings, streets paved with polished cobbles, a Roman archway of massive earth-coloured stones. And through the archway, a piazza, stalls piled high with melons and peaches and apricots, fruit that had ripened naturally, in mellow sunlight, against rose-brick country walls. She imagined she broke open a dusty apricot and saw the insides glow, deeply, translucently rich, in the darkness of her mind. The earthy, apricot smell, pungent and moist, rose up and filled her nostrils. Her mouth watered, longingly.

57

Beyond the sepia-tinted glass of the curved wind-screen the wide sweep of a Roman road led them on, the steel tracks of tramlines cut into blocks of warm granite curving forever before them: the way back to yesterday. Sarah breathed happily. In Italy, the past was so much more ancient, complex, troubled, than her own. And yet these stones endured.

"I should come and live here," she said, watching the campanile, pink and golden against blue sky, flanked by a tall, black cypress and a sentinel umbrella pine.

Tania puffed silently at her small cigar, then stubbed it out, half finished, without comment.

At night they dined at a long trestle table set on the villa's terrace amid private pines that led down to a private sea. It was a motley group, consisting largely of the wives and teenage offspring of very rich men. Only two of the men concerned were present: Tania's small, burly, aggressive husband, Mort, who had grown up in Brooklyn and made his first fortune in American real estate, and a grey-haired man called Ben. They ate Parma ham and melon, and disposed of tureen upon tureen of succulent mussels, mopping the sauce up with chunks of crisp Italian bread, piling the gleaming empty shells back into the huge white bowls.

Conversation occurred in little flurries: whispers and giggles among the teenagers, brief flares of anger, the occasional dangerous cross-generational debate. Tania sat across from Sarah, sharing her shawl with a nine-year-old neighbour: she'd always had a talent for the picturesque. With her mock-wild hair drawn up into a demure top-knot, her childishly shirred sundress compressing her tiny breasts, her bright, mischievous eyes and coquettish laugh, Tania made the child, an overweight person with a stolid, knowing face, look positively middle-aged.

Tania's own children were up the other end of the table, arguing with their father: Daniel, a dark, curly-haired Murillo boy poised over the grapes, and Natalie, a large, ungainly girl wearing a smock and an anxious-to-please frown between her eyes. The Monster, their father, growled and sneered as drugs were discussed, and VD, and education; money and cars and motor boats, the virility of yachts and knots. His exaggerated snarls successfully aborted a promising discussion of feminism in Italy, now.

"Gentlemen beware!" warned the Monster. "With only two men round this table, we're outnumbered five to one."

"Young Daniel's a man," Tania taunted from her end of the table. "Even if he is your son."

The Monster spat in the direction of his handsome child. "That's not a man, it's a mouse."

Daniel peeled grapes as expertly as he ignored the jibe.

"A man on the beach told Natalie what a beautiful body she'd got," said Tania, pursuing her own, curious flirtation with the man she loved to hate. She threw a tender glance at her lumpy daughter, who blushed and looked away.

The Monster's furious little eyes disappeared into his brows with anger. "What, that great, fat, slobby lump of shapeless flesh?" he roared. Natalie got up and left the table, cheeks burning, eyes bright with hurt, and held-back tears. Tania pushed her chair back and prepared to follow her.

"Darling?"

It was a warning so powerful that Sarah thought she had never heard so much threat in a voice as Mort packed into that lovely and innocent endearment.

"Sit down!" He thumped the table. Cups and saucers jumped, and a wine bottle slid off and shattered on the tiles of the terrace floor. Tania sat down.

"They've got to learn to take it," he said to those assembled. "Even kids. Even girls. Where would I be if I hadn't learned to take knocks?" He banged the table again, to emphasise "knocks", and Sarah felt sure she could hear her own teeth rattle in her head.

The Monster raised his head from the creases of his neck, a bull scenting danger, and glared challengingly at the scared faces round his table. "I'd certainly not be here," he roared, sniffing the private air, indicating the pines and the private sea. The candles nearest him flickered wildly for a moment, throwing weird shadows, fire before a storm.

"Can money buy love, do you think?" Sarah asked, in as chatty a tone of voice as she could manage.

"Round here, it can," young Daniel said unexpectedly. "We see it everywhere."

"Money seduces people, so they fall in love." It was Tania speaking. "And the love they fall into doesn't always go away." She gazed at the Bully placatingly across the table. "Success is a powerful aphrodisiac," she said, almost pleadingly. She meant: "I chose you. I'll stay with you. Please don't beat me up tonight."

60

"Women are naturally drawn to power," the Monster growled. "The strong always attract the weak. Women are not only weak, they're inferior to men in every way." He snorted again with his own peculiarly raucous brand of derisive laughter. "I trust everyone agrees."

Once again, he glared around the table, making sure that every man, woman and child was in his thrall. "What these feminist women need," he declared, "what every woman needs, is a good old-fashioned fuck."

With a shock Sarah realised that Mort meant every word he said. There was silence for a moment. People sat as if hypnotised, unable to imagine what might happen next.

The terrace by the sea, the whispering pines, the balmy, velvet Italian night, were the setting for a fairy tale, but the one to be enacted was Beauty and the Beast, a story full of menace.

Each day the Beast rampaged round the extent of his estates, wreaking havoc everywhere. Scorching with his breath, trampling with his hoofs, lunging and plunging and piercing and goring with his horns. Destroying. Raping and looting and pillaging and laying waste. And at the end of every day Beauty, his poor child-wife, hid in her bed chamber, cowering at each roar, and dreading the night to come.

Sarah raised her eyes and found the finger of the Beast pointing at her.

"You, too, Sarah. That's what you need, too. A good old-fashioned fuck would sort you out."

★

61

Tania found Sarah at the sea's edge in darkness, a little later, sitting on some worn stone steps. She was having what old-fashioned once-a-week movie-goers described as "a jolly good cry".

"I certainly never thought this week's weepie would be the story of my own true life," she sniffed, mopping her face with the tissues Tania proffered and finding that the smallness of someone's arms in no way diminished the powerful comfort of a hug.

"I'm sorry if all that – crudeness – upset you, Sarah. But you know Mort. He's always offending people, and he doesn't mean a word of it."

"I think he does," said Sarah. "The fact is that he knew me with Adam. And if Adam had been here, or absent but alive, Mort would never have said that to me. Not in a million years. You don't say things like that to married ladies."

"It's especially cruel to give that advice to someone who's recently widowed," Tania said. "He never thinks about the person he's speaking to. But I can't think of you as a social outcast. You usually seem so independent, so able to cope."

"The truth is, I'm unprotected," said Sarah. "And still in a state of shock. Do you know I have to hold on to the banisters when I go downstairs? I can't just run down like I used to do. It's knocked my coordination for six."

"I should think it would," said Tania. "But that won't last. And at least you've had some practice in going out in company alone."

"Adam travelled such a lot. But I never dined with couples who invited me out of pity. Ugh!"

"You always seemed very much yourself, Sarah, never just half of a couple."

"Huh! *Seemed!*" said Sarah. "I might have seemed independent. In lots of ways I suppose I was. But not of him. I married too young for that. We formed one another, Adam and I. We grew up, or brought ourselves up, together."

She grabbed Tania by the shoulders and shook her passionately. "That's why I need, now, to stand on my own two feet! Don't you see? I can't run the risk of living through anyone else again."

Tania watched the light of a lone fishing boat disappearing out of sight. "You can't live anyone else's life for them, can you?" she sighed. "I do wish, as women, we weren't programmed so effectively to try."

The water lapped ceaselessly against the ancient steps, slowly wearing away the stone.

"That's my idea of sin," Sarah said. "Mortal sin. A sin against the unique, the individual character of our nature."

Tania was silent for a moment, then she said softly: "At least you didn't have an identity crisis, Sarah, like most widows have when they're first bereaved. You never had to ask yourself who you were, now you were no longer Mrs. Adam Cornish."

"No, I was lucky there. My job gave me a name and an identity. So I'm able to mourn the real loss, the loss of Adam, and all the things he was, and not the loss of my own identity or status."

A fresh breeze came up, stirring the pines to a rasping restlessness, and Sarah longed with a fierce longing to be with David now, to go into his room and watch him sleeping, to cover him gently with the bedclothes he'd managed to get tangled round his feet.

And she wanted, too, to hear the subtle magic of

Rob's voice telling her the day's disasters, making her laugh at some story of a buzzard and an old witch and a prophecy; or a farmer who couldn't shear his sheep. She wouldn't sleep unless she heard Rob's voice. You never knew, he might also say he loved her.

"I'd like to make a couple of calls home," she said. "Would Mort object? I'd pay for them, of course."

"That's fine. You could have them for free if it were up to me," said Tania. "But so many people take advantage of Mort. His family. Even his oldest friends. And he *is* self-made, you know."

"I'm on expenses," Sarah said. "Thank goodness I am. I couldn't afford to travel, otherwise."

They walked back arm in arm towards the house and Sarah thought she felt Tania shiver as they entered the shadow the building cast so blackly across the moonlit peace. Exposed, she may be. And unprotected. But Sarah had no fears like Tania's fears. She had very little fear at all, now that she'd had to face the horror most wives fear. Tania was hugely protected from the outside world, she was financially and socially secure, and look at the price she had to pay.

I'd never pay that price, thought Sarah.

"I spent half the night thinking of wittily devastating retorts I should have made to Mort," Sarah said, chuckling, as she and Tania walked along the beach next day. "In better times I'd never have let him get away with it. Do you really think men believe that simplistic stuff about a good fuck? They're always saying it."

"The trouble is, it's too darn often true," said Tania.

64

"I can't remember the last time I had a good one, can you?"

Sarah looked at her in astonishment. "Don't you sleep with Mort?" she asked. "Don't you, um, make love?"

Tania walked on in front, along a narrow strand between rocks, flinging her words backwards to Sarah on the scented wind. "I'm such a fool," she said. "I try and try to get affection from him. And all I get is hurt."

"You haven't answered the question."

"We have separate bedrooms. We had so many violent rows, you see, it's better that way. I couldn't bear it, the way he rolled over and wouldn't touch me, afterwards."

Beauty provoking the Beast. Beauty wooing the loathsome Beast. Learning to conquer her fear of his size and his ugliness and all his ferocity. Hanging her little arms round his terrible neck: once you pluck up your courage and dare to kiss the Beast, he turns into a Prince. And we all live happily ever after.

And so, Tania had loved her Beast, tended him, cared for him, and waited patiently. One night she would catch him removing his woolly, pantomime-Monster's mask. Surely he couldn't sleep in that thing? It was a simple matter of keeping herself awake. But try as she might, she never did catch the Monster without his snout. Year after year she waited for all that terrible gruffness to change into warm affection, but the Beast was not transformed. Nobody was transformed. And she was always so tired these days, she could not keep awake. Perhaps she hadn't loved him hard enough? She renewed her efforts, twisting her fragile body into servile positions to please the Beast, bearing him children, smiling and smiling, and looking away when it was necessary to look away. But still his hoofs trampled her, and his clumsy, vice-strong grasp left marks all over her, indelible marks, the marks of the Beast. He had a most particular way of being unpleasant, he had perfected it and it was peculiar to the Beast himself: he was passionately unpleasant.

Every day and every night she was tormented by the ugliness of his behaviour, but still she would not give up hope that one day he would be transformed.

"My behaviour can be explained in terms of the classic personality breakdown syndrome." Unlikely words to be flung backwards on the warm sea-breath of an Italian wind.

Sarah had quite forgotten that Tania was studying psychology and was, at present, deeply "into" social institutions. A late twentieth-century Beauty, married to a medieval Beast, she had fought Mort all the way over her right to go back to college, and finish her degree, and now she was doing a correspondence course for an extra diploma in the social sciences.

"Think of the camps, and of prisons," she said now, gravely, as they sat down on a seaweed-laden rock and dangled their legs in the sea. "People are stripped of their belongings, torn away from their loved ones and all that was familiar to them, deprived of privacy, subjected to constant harassment and constant cruelty. They are made to do menial work, deprived of so much as a moment a day alone. What happens? They lose their identity. They become dependent on those being cruel to them because They are Authority. You can't trust the cruel ones, but there is no one else to trust.

"There's no such thing as autonomy anymore; you can't even talk for fear of being overheard. A moment's kindness makes you grovel with gratitude, even love. You take on the personality of those in authority, wear bits of their clothing. (I often wear Mort's dressing gown.) You emulate their ways."

Sarah listened, amazed. Tania no longer spoke in her breathless, childish voice, the voice she had used last night, her Monster-placating voice. "It's not far-fetched at all," this new, strong-minded Tania was insisting. "It's quite a good analogy. Look what happened to me. When I was institutionalised. Does it matter that the institution I am in is known as 'marriage'?

"I was taken away from my family, a warm and loving family, as you know. I was removed from my familiar home, and all my friends, from my life at the university – and remember, Sarah, I was still in my first year. I was stripped of everything, while my parents looked on and smiled. My identity was removed: they even took my name."

The Bride Stripped Bare of Her Bachelors, Even.

"And what was I given in return? A poky little house, a husband I neither knew nor understood, and, after ten months, a tiny baby who terrified the daylights out of me. Do you know, Sarah, I cried every day for a year? Only when *he* was out, of course. He never knew. I hid everything from him. Even two nervous breakdowns."

"You who were always so open," said Sarah. "But

67

why do you stay? For God's sake, Tania, I don't understand."

"I'm trapped, don't you see?" Tania said simply.
"As much by compassion as by lack of money of my
own. Of course, you wouldn't know about that. You've
always worked. All the time you were married to
Adam, you always had a job that paid a living wage."

Sarah thought she detected resentment in Tania's
voice.

"You can't know what it's like to be financially
dependent on your husband," Tania went on. "The
horror of it. To be given presents you don't need, but
to have to ask for the most basic of necessities. And all
this has happened to me because I made the decision all
women are programmed to make: I married at nineteen
and immediately had a child. You weren't trapped,
Sarah, because you postponed having your child and
went on working after most women in your peer group
had given up."

This time, the resentment in Tania's voice was
obvious.

"You make it sound as if I postponed the child on
purpose," Sarah said. "But it is true that the accident of
not getting pregnant in the first years of my marriage
helped me to establish myself at work. What's extraordinary, I suppose, is that, in spite of a career which
enabled me to be financially independent, I should still
be finding the other kinds of independence, the social
and spiritual ones, so difficult."

"Things may have changed a bit," said Tania. "But
it's still hard for women to act aggressively, to speak
out, to put themselves first. The studies of women in
therapy reveal that, time and time again."

"We have to learn how to do that. Men find it natural. We're talking about power, I suppose."

"And money is its metaphor," said Tania, feelingly. "I mean I know it sounds crazy for me to be short of money when Mort's made so much of the stuff, but down here, I'm surrounded by other women who feel the same. It's awful, I know. It's worse than that – it's shocking. How to put up with your husband, for his money, is our favourite coffee-morning topic-of-conversation. It's a clear-cut power situation. The wives of rich men seldom have any access to their money. Even their jewels aren't usually their own."

"I thought you had money of your own when you married him."

"I gave it to him to invest for me. And now it's in 'our' name."

"You could work, you know." Sarah tried to keep the level of irony in her voice acceptably low.

"What could I work at that would keep me in stockings, Sarah, as our mothers used to say? I'd love to work. But it's too late, I think. Unless my degree qualifies me for research. There's an age limit on any job I'm fitted for. And besides, I'd have to move back to London without Mort and live entirely on the miserable salary I could earn."

"I'm not impressed," said Sarah. "It sounds to me as if you *want* to be dependent. You wallow in it. I suspect what you'd really like, deep down, is to meet someone else."

"You're right," said Tania, shamelessly. "I think of it all the time. I have dreams that I pass this place, walking by on the beach path with someone's arm around me. Affectionately. You know, round my shoulders, holding me, so I feel really safe. It's so strange, Sarah, I always wake up from those dreams in tears. I'm desperately sorry for Mort, you see. It's not his fault that he's so aggressive. That he can't give affection and finds it difficult to love. I have to comfort him."

"What on earth for, Tania? For being so horrid to you?"

"I have to reassure him, all the time. He's so terribly insecure. There are all the usual reasons. You can't blame people, can you, for what was done to them? The imprinting, and all that."

They walked to the village and sat at the café sipping *granitas* through straws. Expensive yachts winked their polished brasses at them, their owners concentrating on important matters, like the daily expansion of the muscles in their chests.

"In the beginning, Mort wanted to get rich in order to rescue his mother from his brute of a father," Tania said. "Then she went and died before he could rescue her, so all his riches seemed pointless. Now he can't even rescue himself. All he can do is prevent my escape. And put me down in public all the time, so no one else will want me. Well, perhaps, when the children are older. Who knows what will happen then?"

Tania stared at the fishing boats out at sea as if willing one of them to sail up and rescue her.

Sarah paid the bill and got up from the table.

"I have to go," she said. "Last night Mel woke David to speak to me. He's missing me. He wants me to come home. If I leave now, I can pick him up and get him home to his own bed before bedtime."

"Thank goodness for David," Tania said. "Without

him you'd have absolute freedom, and absolute freedom destroys absolutely."

"There's no such thing," Sarah said. "And certainly not for me. Not yet. I'm still a long way from being free of my marriage, and I want and don't want to be free of Adam."

"David's your centre. He pulls you home, where you're needed."

"Yes. Without him, I'd have no home at all."

5

When she arrived at Mel's, it was Mel she hugged and held on to, not David, for David was being off-hand, much too off-hand, in the background.

"He's been fine," said Mel, leading Sarah to a chair and pushing her into it. "Happy as a sand-boy. It only happened this afternoon."

Sarah's stomach contracted, churned, turned itself inside out. "What happened?"

"I don't know, really. We picked him up from school, as usual. They had their tea. They went out into the garden to play. One of the older girls, Elizabeth, seems to have upset him." Mel caught the look on Sarah's face. "For God's sake, Sarah, it's not your fault. That sort of thing happens whether you're here or not." She sighed. "Oh, guilt! The most useless emotion in the world. I quote *you*, in calmer days."

Sarah sipped the "toothcurler" Mel had poured her and made a face.

"Elizabeth and Tina were practising somersaults, handstands, cartwheels, that sort of thing. They're very competitive, those two – "

"That's it," said Sarah. "David hates things like that. He hates turning upside down." She looked up at Mel without seeing, remembering her own, unathletic childhood. "Come to think of it, so did I. Long jump, high jump, running, fine – but hanging from the parallel bars, face downwards – ugh." She shuddered at the thought. "I've often wondered if it was because I grew upside down in my mother's womb and they couldn't turn me. The breech position, they call it."

"But David wasn't?"

"No. I suppose they made fun of his fears?"

"Of course. Don't make a heavy of it, Sarah. He'll get over it."

Sarah made an effort to smile. "The question is, will I?" she said, wryly.

David paid great attention to the bears and squares as they walked home from the bus. With hard-won restraint Sarah forbore to question him, to hug him, to demonstrate. They were almost at their own front door when he kicked a pebble past her, and said suddenly, "The world looks funny upside down. The grass goes on and on and you can't see any sky." He looked at her challengingly. "It gives me a nasty feeling," he said.

After supper, Sarah washed up, remembering the revelation she had had, about six weeks after Adam's death, over this same sink. She had looked into the detergent foam, which was singularly lacking that day in any rainbow colours, and suddenly thought: "But *he* doesn't know." At once she felt ten years younger and three stones lighter. "It's only me who has to bear it. Adam doesn't *know* that he has died. He never felt the tragedy, never mourned or pined or fretted at the loss of his young life, his talents all unused. I don't have to carry it for him. I don't have to suffer the weight of that appalling sadness. He didn't know the sadness. I need only cope with me, David-and-me, our loss, our grief."

She experienced again the great weight lifting from her body as the words of this humdrum revelation repeated themselves to her. She was buoyed up by a sense of relief, a heady sense of lightness. She smiled. If it's only my pain, she said to herself, then perhaps I can cope.

She turned from the sink to wipe her hands, and saw David. He was standing with his back to her, and his head against the kitchen wall. He was holding his body unnaturally still. She stood a few feet from him, and watched him warily. Every muscle in her ached to take him in her arms and she knew she must not. The child made a strange sound in his throat, like an old man's smoking cough.

"I don't think we can manage without Daddy," he said, in a tight little voice.

Sarah reeled. Her stomach ached as if she had been punched. Her heart pounded at double its usual speed. Her eyes welled. She took a few moments to recover her voice, and a few more moments to respect David's privacy, that space around him which seemed to echo with pain.

Then, as evenly as she could, she said: "No, I don't think we can."

He wheeled around and stared at her in surprise. His all-powerful mother had admitted it. Truly, the world was upside down. He watched her, as she collapsed into a kitchen chair and held out her arms to him. He came to her then, and she held him on her lap while he sobbed the terrible sobs, his head buried in her shoulder, the whole of his small body shaking, his scalding tears seeping through her skin, salting her bloodstream, silting up her heart. Her own tears dropped, unheeded on

74

his head. She rocked him as if he were still a baby. She was rocking herself.

After a while, his weeping stopped. He sniffed determinedly, pulled his head away and looked at her.

"But we have to?" he asked, lips trembling, the question mark wobbling in his voice. She didn't answer, and her silence vibrated a long moment between them. "That's what you always say," he added, at last, resentfully.

Words reverberated, the banal dialogues of the bereaved.

How can you bear it? people had asked her over and over again in the early days, a hint of reproach in the voice, amazed – as she was herself – by the sheer, inane fact of her survival. She caught them glancing at her, then turning superstitiously away. She had looked the thing in the face, one could see the awful power of it in her eyes. They did not want to guess what dark and fearful features she'd been condemned to see. And once seen, changed for ever.

They moved away from her a little as they spoke – it was understandable, after all. Perhaps death was contagious. Someone who'd seen, touched, smelled the unimaginable could be carrying the germ; such terrible knowledge might rub off on one. And so she had answered them impatiently.

"I can't bear it. But I have to."

There was no alternative. She was left alive.

She kissed the damp top of David's head.

"Seems like it," she said.

We bear what we have to bear.

★

75

She telephoned Adam's mother, Adela, to see if she was all right. A friend's daughter, in her third year at the Slade, wanted to paint Adela's portrait. Sarah liked the idea very much.

"I refused, of course," the old lady said. "I told her she should do you instead. Who wants to look at an old woman, wrinkled and full of grief?"

Sarah argued for the portrait until she detected something desperate in Adela's voice: the idea of a likeness of herself in paint somehow offended her to the core.

"How can I be painted?" she kept repeating. "I should not even be alive."

A picture of oneself was confirmation of one's existence, Sarah supposed. She'd never thought of it like that before.

"No one wants a picture of the dead," Adela pleaded passionately. "A ghost. A person who is only breathing by mistake."

According to her, They had got it wrong up there, and as soon as They realised, They would rectify the mistake. It was unnatural for a mother to be alive when her only child was dead. It was not in the scheme of things. Had she not carried him tenderly in her womb?

Sarah remembered the day after that most terrible of nights. She had gone to see Adela: there were some things one had to do oneself. Adela had opened the door and retreated across the room, then she had watched while Sarah approached. A look Sarah would never forget had crossed her dignified old face. Without a word she had flung herself face downwards on the sofa and curled her large body into a foetal position. "No!" she screamed, pounding her fists into the soft upholstery. "No, no, no."

It had taken two strong neighbours to hold her down, as she gasped piteously for breath. And then the doctor administered his shot.

In the event, Sarah had not had to tell Adela anything.

She telephoned her own mother to see if she was all right.

"Where have you been?" sniffed Dolly resentfully. "Somewhere nice?"

"I've been staying with Tania, in Italy."

Her mother sucked in her breath. "All those rich people," she said, envy coarsening her voice. "Did you meet anyone, dear? I'd so much like you to settle down."

"You mean up, don't you?" said Sarah, unable to avoid the clipped tones of disgust.

"Is it awful to say it? It'll soon be a year, and it's something you'll have to consider, after all." Dolly paused, but Sarah failed to respond. "I only want what's best for you. I'm your mother. Who else could have your best interests at heart?"

"You're there!" pounced Pythagoras. "Wherever have you been? Paris? San Remo? You can't escape from guilt, or grief, however far you run. Do you think that by choosing glitzy places and frivolous lightweight people you can counteract the weights you have to carry?"

"You don't know anything about survival," Sarah said. "I'm just a woman, trying to survive."

"The poor wife's survival kit, they call me. Well, aren't you going to ask me round? Don't want me, eh? Well, that's a sure sign of guilt. What you need, my girl, is old Pythagoras's scientific prick inside you. I have it on Authority. My own. There's no neurosis that can't be cured by a jolly good – "

"Fuck," said Sarah.

A few days later, she went, after work, to a small and elegant hotel in Mayfair where she was due to meet her lawyer and discuss her Will over dinner.

Simon had been up at Oxford with Adam. A vague sort of chap, with sheepish good looks, a lot of charm and an open car (a rare luxury in those days), he had enjoyed an unearned popularity which blossomed each Sunday when he drove a host of fellow students on a pub crawl around the neighbouring riverside inns and taverns where they disported themselves in the ineffably silly way expected of them. An important part of Simon's charm was that no one had ever caught him doing any work, and it was rumoured that he spent his days locked in his rooms reading his way through the great Russian novels instead. Everyone tried to catch him out, on Sundays, by bandying the patronymics of a few minor characters about, but Simon would always deflect these sallies, smiling vaguely and fitting another of someone else's Black Russian Sobranie cigarettes into the silver and tortoise-shell holder he'd inherited – a bemused character of unimpeachable dimness, out of Wodehouse.

In the same vague way, Simon had officiated at Sarah

and Adam's wedding, the Best Man best qualified to see that everyone got a lift to the reception in someone else's car.

Failing to enter the real grown-up world when he came down, Simon had become a solicitor, and in the way of these things, had become Sarah and Adam's solicitor, too. Full of a solicitude Sarah could have done without, he had wound up Adam's estate for her and made out all the documents of transfer, whereupon it appeared that Sarah must Make a Will.

At first, Sarah had enjoyed the exercise. She had not been left very much anyway since Adam had been free-lance, so there was no pension or even compensation, and they had not believed in insurance policies – you only win if you die young, had been the joke – and almost all of what she had would go to David, but it was fun planning who she could please with unexpected legacies, or precious objects like small pieces of jewel-lery, or favourite pictures.

She pictured Rob's face when he realised that he had the means to pay almost all his bills and she spent a delightful time puzzling over whether to leave him a lump sum he could squander instantly, or to pay for his fishing rights in advance for thirty years.

There was nothing Sarah liked better than planning presents for the people she loved and if she were going to do such a ridiculous thing as make a Will she sup-posed she had better do it as seriously as if she were to be under that proverbial bus tomorrow.

And it was here, over the question of small legacies, and Sarah's pleasure in them, that Simon had taken issue with her. A Will, he said, was not a matter of sentiment at all. It was not about people or things you loved.

A Will was, very simply, a legal document. He would explain the whole thing to her (in words of one syllable) over a pheasant and a bottle of Gevrey Chambertin.

Sarah had telephoned David from her office, and listened intently for sounds of disquiet in his voice. She'd been reassured – he had his favourite young neighbourhood sitter to stay that night – and her relief had been so great that she had actually arrived early for her date with Simon. She went to the powder room and tidied herself up, then prowled about the mellow, panelled rooms and the bar for all the world as if she were waiting for a lover. Men looked at her and she looked back at them, imperious and unperturbed, every bit as curious, amused and in control as they were.

No Simon. Five minutes still to spare. She settled herself in a deep sofa and rested her head on the back of it so she could study the nicely painted relief work on the ceiling. Snatches of sentences she'd been working on that afternoon repeated themselves in her head. That flourish at the paragraph's end, she had almost got it to work – a quotation, and careful spacing and punctuation – it might, just might, seem unpretentious. How she enjoyed this knitting with words and commas and space, seeing the garment grow. How lucky she was to have work she liked to do, and get reasonably well paid for it. Most young widows with children had no job, no "visible means of support".

"Hello," said Simon, smiling down at her from a great height. How big boned and tall he was! She'd forgotten his size – perhaps he'd put on weight. "No, don't get up. You look so comfortable down there."

He joined her on the sofa and at once drinks and nuts appeared, followed by menus and cigarettes. Apart from the largeness of him, he seemed quite unchanged. He produced the silver and tortoise-shell cigarette holder and lit up, waving the smoke about unselfconsciously, his long, well-shaped hands making surprisingly graceful gestures.

"No Sobranie?" asked Sarah.

Simon smiled. "Duty frees," he explained.

Irrelevantly, Sarah thought of the bomb scare years ago when the Civil Defence people had advocated brown paper bags against nuclear fallout and Simon had ordered his from Harrods. She started to laugh, but Simon didn't notice. He was describing Life to her, and that, too, seemed to come cling-wrapped from Harrods.

Was it possible that such a Wodehousian world existed still? Hampers of caviar and hot toast and cold champagne, picnics on sports days on velvety greensward. Winchester, Charterhouse, Christ Church – The House itself. Motors with sycamore dashboards or walnut facings, their interiors smelling warmly of leather and cigars. Strawberries and cream and punts among willows and Beaumes de Venise and sons who are sent on the grand European Tour until Dad can pull strings of the right length at his old college . . . Simon glanced at Sarah for a moment – and she saw stark incredulity in his half closed eyes.

"These days one has to pull strings," he told her.

A tray of plump-breasted grouse went by, exquisitely prepared and dressed. They moved to their reserved corner table in the dining room, and ordered grouse. While Simon tasted the previously opened Gevrey Chambertin, Sarah disturbed his concentration by remembering how sick they all used to get at parties on

Entre deux Mers. Simon looked pained at this mention of the messy vulgarities of childhood, took another sip, rolled it carefully around his tongue, and looked pained indeed. Beckoning the wine waiter, he examined the bottle's label and cork.

"I thought so!" he thundered, while the poor man quivered. "The wrong year!" They drank a superb Aloxe Corton instead.

"Oxford became the time of *l'entre deux mers* to Adam and me," Sarah said, ignoring the flinch invariably produced in Adam's old friends when she mentioned his name in so natural and jolly a manner. "A pun on Eliot – 'And in the time of *l'entre deux guerres.*'"

Simon frowned and produced a folded, typewritten slip from his wallet. "I wrote this on holiday in Sardinia last week," he said. "It's especially for you." He handed it over as if it were the privy purse.

Sarah unfolded the paper and stared at the three lines perfectly typed upon it. Their burden was couched in so Latinate a manner she could barely comprehend it. Astonished, she looked up at Simon, to see that a lofty smile of self-satisfaction had settled on his features.

"I've needed to formulate this for quite a while," he told her. "A lot of people – old people, women – make your mistake. They think a Will is a matter of senti-ment, of emotion, and worse still, they clutter it with *things*." He shuddered. "A Will, as I've pointed out here, is never a matter of sentiment. A Will is entirely a legal affair."

She looked from his face to the paper again, amazed. "What language is this in?" she queried. "It's not in English, that's for sure." She began to correct the grammar.

Simon smiled patiently at her and poured some more wine. "We get lots of them, dotty old ladies," he explained in a kindly tone. "Leave all their money to 365 different cats' homes. And we have to sort out the mess. It won't do, you know. Straightforward family Wills are the only acceptable thing. This kind of nonsense gives a lawyer a lot of trouble." He paused. "It could even make him a laughing stock in the courts. Why, a judge could criticise me for even allowing a Will like yours to be drawn up."

Speechless, Sarah stared at him, then took a gulp of wine. "Simon," she said dangerously, "I am not yet a dotty old lady. Or hadn't you noticed?"

Simon ignored her and went straight on. "Lists of gifts are not for Wills," he intoned. "When people leave messy Wills like this – and it's almost always women – their friends laugh all the way to the bank. You can't leave things to *friends*."

"Why not?" asked Sarah.

"Look, sometimes men leave money to their mistresses. We tell them they're misguided, but they insist on it. And we all laugh. Poor fools! Anyone can see those women don't care. Out for the main chance, every one of them. No, family's the only thing. You can never be sure about friends."

"I can."

"They're taking you for a ride."

"My friends are my family."

The sweet trolley arrived and Simon chose the fresh cream trifle. "Coffee," said Sarah. "Hot and black." She longed for it to arrive.

"I've seen too many of these things," continued Simon. "You'd have to have read Law like I did at

Oxford and had twenty years' experience in practice to understand. It's quite simply imprudent to bequeath money outside the family. Imprudent and impractical. There was one old lady I remember who'd found 100 different charities – some of them weren't even registered." He contemplated his trifle in disgust. "They were people who'd come to her door and asked for money, the local convent, that sort of thing. She didn't even have their addresses."

"And what did you do?"

"Oh, we got her to cut the list by about half, and made sure who they were."

"You mean, made sure you approved."

"This is getting acrimonious, Sarah, and we don't want that." A blob of cream and custard trembled for a moment on his lip. "You won't have enough to leave David as it is. You have to estimate that estates are generally cut in half – taxes, and death duties, and – "

"Lawyers' fees?"

Simon paused and glared at her, then pointed at the slip of paper lying next to the after dinner mints. "I've broken my rule tonight," he said stiffly.

"What rule is that?"

"Never to explain the same thing more than one way."

Should she find another lawyer, someone who wouldn't patronise her? Or should she just coldly see to it that Simon did her will. And her Will?

"You're in a very unusual situation," he continued.

"Oh, why's that? Because I'm in control? In charge of my own affairs, my own destiny? And because I know exactly what I'm doing?"

"Well, women don't often make decisions of this kind entirely on their own."

"I see. I've got this power accidentally – and you're here to see I don't exercise it without masculine advice. How dare you presume to tell me who I love, and who loves me?"

"Yes. Well," said Simon, retreating behind the best most bemused of manners, and rising to his feet. "I've seldom had so difficult an encounter in such congenial surroundings, over so pleasant a meal."

He glanced round at the dining room with its snowy linen and silver trolleys, its ancient male retainers and male guests talking to one another in hushed respectful tones.

Following his glance Sarah noticed for the first time that she was in enemy territory. They had got her surrounded, too. There was not another woman in the place.

6

"Amazing, isn't it," said Colin, "how secret Cornwall still is. I mean, look at us, tunnelling along these green lanes enclosed by tall hedges and low trees that meet and intertwine at the top. And beside us flows an unseen river, silently creeping into a hidden creek . . . "

"Smugglers' territory," Sarah said, amused. "How lyrical you are. What relish in your description of the secretive. You like secrets, don't you, Colin?"

"I seem to like telling you mine," Colin said, his exquisite lip curving under his perfectly trimmed moustache, the colour rising becomingly to his handsome blond cheek.

Thank goodness they'd taken a local driver, who knew the terrain, Sarah thought, as they snaked along merrily round hairpin bends barely visible in the leaf green light. Nothing was as it seemed. Colin was not the dashing young cavalry officer he appeared to be, but an excellent photographer, who had accompanied her on an assignment of interviews in St. Ives.

"Oh, I've been so promiscuous," Colin sighed, with relish, adjusting the tilt of his brown felt trilby, while Sarah admired the shape of his head and the beautiful cut of his buttercup yellow hair. They were wasted, nowadays, such gorgeous young men: she'd like to have seen Colin as a chocolate box soldier in high boots, a sword and lots of gaudy braid.

"I never enjoyed it, of course," he was saying. "One's Puritan background sees to that."

"Always boys?"

"Except for my marriage, which was pretty brief. Oh, Sarah. If only you'd seen me with Kofi, he was the only one I loved. He was so black, and I'm so fair, we were spectacular together. We'd come into a party and everything would stop. I wanted to photograph us making love on satin sheets, but I never did. I could have sold those photos for a fortune." He sighed again. "I tried to commit suicide when he left. They only just rescued me in time."

"Oh, Colin – "

"I've had two escapes, both narrow ones," he said. "But I might try again, some time. Don't look so horrified. It would make no difference to anything if I died."

"Oh, yes, it would," Sarah began as the car came to an abrupt stop, and the driver confessed with bewilderment to being lost. "It's a tiny inn, right at the end of the creek," she explained.

"There's nothing but unmade road from here," said the driver, grumpily. Sarah persuaded him to take the unmade road.

"We're up shit creek, all right," said Colin, starting to giggle.

"Without the proverbial paddle."

"Speak for yourself. There's a paddle right here but girls can't play with it."

They stopped with a jolt at the door of a quaint old inn.

★

87

Graceful *copitas* of sherry in hand, they stood by a curved bow window like characters in a Coward play.

"Did you hear what they said?" Colin said for the third time, giggling delightedly. "Would you and your *wife* like a sherry?"

Outside, the river grew dark as oil and the masts of small craft bobbed and swayed and the trees tossed restlessly, whispering amongst themselves, waiting for the secrets of another night. A smell of country river damp rose up, together with other, unexpected smells. Colin sniffed appreciatively. "What's that, Sarah? Butter (sniff). Oh, tarragon (sniff) – it must be *béarnaise*. We're over the kitchen, I suppose. They can obviously cook."

"Onions," sniffed Sarah, "bacon, garlic, wine – *coq au vin!*" They groaned and licked their lips. "Or maybe a *daube – provençale*, of course!"

"And mint, fresh mint, just chopped. And what's that rhubarb smell? Fool, d'you think? Or pudding? Or rhubarb tart. With a sprinkling of ginger, to be served with lashings of cream. It's not fair," Colin salivated. "You'll have a super meal, and I bet that unpredictable boyfriend of yours won't arrive till midnight, and you'll have to eat alone."

"Then stay," said Sarah. Rob had already left one message for her saying he'd been detained. For all she knew he wouldn't make it till tomorrow morning. "Honestly, Colin, no one at the office will mind if you miss another day. We know that the pictures you got are good."

He frowned at her, though she could see how pleased he was at her suggestion. That pink skin and that carefully trimmed hair – that small moustache. He was conscientious to a fault – he must *work*.

"Is there a buffet car on your train?" she asked.

"Shouldn't think so," said Colin gloomily. "It'll be white bread sandwiches and plastic cups of instant coffee. If we're lucky."

"Stay and have dinner with me. It'll be such fun. You can sleep in my room. They've given me a suite."

He looked at her, entranced, and she moved towards him, longing to touch the curve of his shiny yellow head.

"Besides, it's so safe. You can sleep in my bed, if you like, and I'll cuddle you." She laughed. It would serve Rob right if he arrived and found Colin there. She pictured the scene. Rob would never believe it was innocent. They never did. Even if the man was gay. "I won't seduce you if you don't seduce me? Okay?"

He drew a long breath. "Shall I stay?"

The rumble of wheels on the gravel. "Your carriage awaits, M'sieur."

I don't think I like this play. More Rattigan than Coward, taking Colin through the dark, damp countryside to a dim-lit train, and tomorrow an office, a darkroom, a meeting, a schedule, another meeting. And she to a lonely meal among couples and candlelight, with proprietors clucking: "He'll never make the train. He left it much too late. No, the Chateaubriand's for two. So's the duck *à l'orange*, I'm afraid."

A call in the midst of her chicken (for one) with *béarnaise*. The cosy couples stared as she went to the telephone.

"I got held up," said Rob. "There was a crisis here."

What else was new? "I'm setting out now, but I have to go all the way round a very deep creek to get to you, when in daylight you go across by ferry. It's the end of the earth. You couldn't have chosen a more difficult place to be. I warn you, it's likely to take hours and hours. Especially in the dark." She put the proprietor's lady on to give him precise directions – a route, times, landmarks that show up at night.

"Sorry you have to eat alone," said the lady, coming to Sarah's table, oozing sympathy and thinking there's got to be something wrong with this young woman: one chap leaves her for the train, even though it's much too late to catch it, while another sets out too late to join her. "It's so hard to find us in the dark," she said, accepting a glass of the Sancerre Sarah had ordered.

"Oh, he's a brilliant driver," Sarah said. "He'll find it. Besides, he's not a foreigner, he's a Cornishman himself."

"But not from *these* parts."

Sarah knew how it would be. He'd get too tired to drive. He'd pull off the road somewhere, sleep for an hour in the car, arrive cramped and cross. Why did she bother with Rob? It was difficult to explain. Was it because he was so unlike Adam that she was in no danger of considering him a replacement? Was it because he was lightness itself, if not lightweight, where Adam had been strong and serious? Adam had never once failed to arrive on a plane at a Greenwich Mean Time he'd cabled her with from the ends of the earth whereas Rob was unreliable; and instead of Adam's single-minded drive and application, Rob expected mere vanity to propel him towards his goals. He was no threat to Adam's memory, but offered her a clear contrast: a totally different, carefree kind of life, a whole new set of interests, young, silly and full of laughter. Rob took her "out of herself", and his country world, with its constant rhythm of rebirth and renewal, echoed her hungry desire for life in the face of death.

And so she was often to be found in seductive settings such as these, waiting for Rob. What was it they had said about Errol Flynn in Hollywood? "You always knew precisely where you stood with Errol. In any situation, you knew he would always let you down."

"Could we keep some food for him?"

They gave her an elegant tray in her room. Fresh Cornish crab and mayonnaise, salad and strawberries, all covered tightly with cling-film, mineral water, wine.

"He'll be very late. I'll go to bed," she said. "If you don't mind I'll leave a note on the door to guide him to my room."

The note was so idiotic it had to have an envelope. Unaware of its content, the proprietor's lady fixed it to the door of the inn with a piece of magic putty.

"Now you have driven halfway round the world," she had written, "scaled the fortress, cut down the 100-year hedge, swum the moat, fixed the drawbridge and battered down the gates, it only remains for you to come up the stairs, go through the small sitting room at the top and open my door."

She slept in her four-poster bed and at two a.m. the door opened and the curly head appeared.

"Where are you?" he said, groping for her in the dark, kissing her ear. "You're lost in that bed. Mmmm.

You smell nice." He examined the room in the half-dark, opened a window, drank some mineral water and complained that the place was "horribly twee". He undressed and climbed into bed and wound his cold legs round hers. "Cats' eyes and crossroads and hairpin bends are buzzing in my head," he said. He put his arm round her and fell asleep.

There were strawberries on blue china on the breakfast tray, but Rob seemed anxious to get out.

"Tourist stuff," he remarked disparagingly. "Let's get you back to real country. Let's see some sky."

"Wait – I must phone the office before I leave." She got through to London easily, listened in silence for a minute or two, then covered the mouthpiece with her hand, and said to Rob, "Colin's train has been in a crash. The sleepers were hit the worst. Some of them went up in flames. Oh, Rob. He was in a sleeper."

She was dazed. She sat on the window seat where he'd sat ("Would you and your wife like a sherry?") and cried. "We talked about death sitting here – his death," she told Rob. "He said it wouldn't make any difference to anything if he died."

The dashing young cavalry officer, the brown felt trilby, the smell of *coq au vin*. Those sleepers were like metal cells, you'd be burned alive. They locked you in for safety. You couldn't get out until the train had stopped. No handle on the insides of the door. So stupid. They ought to change the design. She imagined Colin struggling with the lock.

"I must have been the last person – I mean friend – to see him alive," she said. "What is it about me? Maybe it really does rub off and I'm fatal to people – a gruesomely genuine *femme fatale*." She pushed her hands through her hair, then sniffed her fingertips. "Perhaps it's a smell. Wherever I go Death seems to haunt me, follow me. I can't get away from it. And to think he almost missed that train! I could have persuaded him to stay. I tried. I said stay, stay the night. Why didn't I try harder? But he had to go. You know Colin, he had to get to work."

"Let's get you to Merlin country," said Rob. "Let's get you home." He hugged her hard and put her in the car and as she looked at that absurdly romantic profile of his, where all that was sensitive still warred with so much aggression and so much determination, she thought, not for the first time, I love this man. He seems to understand about grief.

They began the journey to Rob's house through sun-lit tunnels of green. She settled back in her seat and he put on his favourite Handel, and after a while he forded a stream where water plumed up in crystal jets in the sunlight and low-lying branches just skimmed the roof of the car.

"What was the crisis yesterday?" she asked idly. "The one that made you late last night. You don't have quite so many crises now the Susies aren't battering at your door." Susie was her collective name for Rob's collected girlfriends.

"Susie did come down," he grinned. "She was doing a spot of riding locally. I had to get rid of her before I could start out for you."

"You're joking."

"I'm not. I wouldn't have told you, but you asked."

They began to climb a hill. "I want to show you something," he said.

An avenue of oaks planted long ago on the brow of a hill, great woolly sheep rubbing themselves against the comforting bark of them, and the valley seen magically through a veil of leaves in all its calm and misty promise. They stood, not touching, by the trunk of a massive oak and, in spite of everything, were together as they had seldom been together. Birdsong sounded loud in the deep tranquillity and Rob identified several songs for her. They absorbed the peace for a while, breathing it in as deeply as they could, storing it in their bloodstreams as if it were wine to be laid lovingly in a cellar and drunk long years ahead in celebration of great feats of love. Then they drove down into the mystic valley which hid in its bosom the meanest, ugliest tin-mining town Sarah had ever seen.

They passed the caff and the fish and chip shop and the abattoir; she put her hands over her ears to blot out the cries she thought she could hear from within, but the smell of the place lingered on. They passed the Victorian railway station, unusually large for such a small place. She caught a glimpse of closed trucks heading for the slaughterhouse.

"I left Ange at that station once, in that waiting room," Rob said, a little later. "We were quarrelling quite a bit at that time and she left and made me drive her to the station. Something made me go back after I'd left her and she was still standing there. She hadn't caught the train. She was wearing a big hat I'd bought her, kind of a dark rust red like the jacket you've got on, and under the hat she was crying – her mascara was all streaked down her face. I put her in the car and drove her home. Things were better between us for quite a while after that."

Sarah put her hand on Rob's denimed knee and he covered it for a moment with his own. He swung the car off the road with his usual authority and she glimpsed the white barred gate and the trees tangled in the drive and the pink and blue hydrangeas in front of the grey stone walls.

"I love this house."

"I should think you do."

That night they made love with all the windows open and heard Rob's special owl hooting mournfully from the woods.

The next day was the day of Rob's party. He had been preparing for it for weeks: there were games marked out in the garden, an archery contest set up on the long lawn, and a treasure hunt with carefully worked out clues hidden everywhere. There were stacks of records ready by the record player, glasses hired from the one local pub Rob still had credit in, and crates of booze from the one off-licence (in a village several miles away) where he had not yet run up ugly bills which were quite impossible to pay. Brenda, the local's barmaid, who was willing-for-a-shilling, had been invited as a friend, though Rob expected her to help him keep the drink circulating. He had taken the largest salmon of the catch out of the freezer for Sarah to prepare, and fixed up a barbecue on the terrace for which he had ordered the best local sausages and chops.

Rob held a party every year towards the end of summer, and every year it became more important to him to demonstrate that, despite the rumours of his bankruptcy, and despite the ever growing list of local creditors and outraged husbands, Rob still lived like a country gentleman of private means and knew how to use his house and garden to entertain the locals at a *fête-champêtre* like any other squire. No – better. For Rob had style.

Sarah smiled to herself as she set about steaming the monstrous salmon in a fish kettle she'd ordered once for Rob from an offer in one of the posher Sundays. Like so many other women before her, the first time that Sarah had come to this house and fallen under its spell she had believed, as she was meant to, that it belonged to Rob. Later she discovered that he rented it at a peppercorn rent, complete with grounds, from the lord of the local manor, on whose estate it sat. The rent was, naturally, long overdue, but, notwithstanding, the long-suffering landlord was invited to the party so he could see for himself that the house was lived in in the style to which it should be accustomed. One day perhaps *he'd* have the style to waive Rob's rent.

Turning off the light under the *court bouillon* in which the salmon rested just before it reached the boil, Sarah remembered the time she'd brought down some champagne and they couldn't cool it because he'd sold the fridge the day before to a bloke in the garage up the road.

"Well, I needed some petrol and the bank had bounced my cheque. I know, we'll cool this bubbly in the stream."

That was the time he'd slipped on those treacherous

smooth stones and done his ankle in. And then there was the time when he'd driven her here past the Post Office so she could go in and pay his telephone bill and give them a written assurance she'd underwrite the next before they would reconnect his telephone.

Sarah was quite aware that the man in the Post Office, like all the locals, thought her a fool being taken for a ride. Why should she care? They couldn't know how important it was to her when she was at home alone in London to have his voice beguile her late at night, or to hear what bird had alighted in what tree in the early morning.

Sarah remembered that weekend very well: it was just after they'd first met. They had wandered round the small Cornish town laying in supplies of food extravagant enough to see six people through a siege. The proceedings took on a pattern which Sarah, at that stage, found vastly entertaining: Rob ordered and Sarah paid.

"We mustn't buy anything frozen," he warned her. "Remember, I sold the fridge."

They went past an antique shop with some pretty china in the window. "Don't buy me a plate for the dresser," he said. "I've sold the dresser."

She tried very hard to keep her face straight as she confronted him.

"What else are you going to tell me? You've sold the house and we're spending the night in a caravan?"

"I would sell the house. It would solve all my problems. The fact is, it doesn't belong to me."

Hugging each other, they collapsed into demented laughter in front of the salmon pink corsets displayed in the old-fashioned draper's window.

Sarah made bowls of salad while the salmon cooled, and then she set about skinning it, a glutinous and messy job made sinister by the unblinking eye of the beast which stared at her balefully throughout. Somehow Rob's fee for fishing rights on one of the most expensive stretches of water in the kingdom never went unpaid, a mystery that was debated endlessly in the pubs he'd been thrown out of, and those he had not been thrown out of yet: it remained a mystery even to the water bailiffs he befriended, whose anger at the salmon poachers was never greater than Rob's own.

Searching the various cupboards, some of which obviously hadn't been opened for years, Sarah found the largest platter in the house, a huge oval dish in old English ironstone with a picture of cows grazing in water meadows done in faded shades of blue. She washed it and dried it and slid the salmon on to it, then garnished the moist pink fleshy beauty with slices of cucumber and hard-boiled eggs, adding tomatoes and radishes and sprigs of herbs and quarters of lemons till she'd created quite a still life.

God! she thought, Christ! I've forgotten the Hollandaise. There'd never be time to make it, now. Filled with guilt, she alighted on a jar of reasonable-looking mayonnaise, which she spooned hurriedly into bowls in case Rob should catch her at it, and added as many chopped herbs as there were to be found by the kitchen door. By now, it was much too late to dress but Rob was wearing his oldest, tightest jeans so perhaps it didn't matter if she didn't change out of hers. She brushed her hair and attended to her face, while the strangest collection of people began to arrive.

There were posh locals and pub locals and people who'd driven down from places miles away. There were old schoolfriends of Rob's and old schoolteachers and a great many old flames. The wives had all baked Rob something – a pie, a cake, a quiche – and a great deal of affection was exchanged when these offerings were handed over. Husbands stood by and watched suspiciously.

The games in the garden excited a lot of interest while inside the house the music was loud and people began to dance. Sarah watched the archery for a bit, was tempted to have a go and revealed no natural aptitude. She wandered inside, consumed some cold white wine, was asked to dance and consumed some more white wine. After a while she began to feel empty inside and rather drunk and left the floor in search of food, but found that the feast she had so lovingly prepared had disappeared. The bones of the giant salmon had been picked so clean that their transparent whiteness glistened almost angrily at her, while empty salad bowls and dirty plates, sticky with mayonnaise, were piled up everywhere.

The scene reminded her of children's parties long ago in her own childhood, when austerity meant that the locusts arrived half an hour before time and swept the board in a matter of minutes, down to the last hundred-and-thousand, or jelly-bean. There had been no such childish greed at David's parties, for plentiful food and sweet things had ceased to be treats. She picked up a fork and speared a last, dejected lettuce leaf, sampled half a mouthful of her special potato salad and collapsed into an old winged chair where she sat, half hidden for a bit, watching the proceedings, somewhat hazily.

She didn't see much of Rob, he was much too busy playing the debonair host, but she caught glimpses of him as he darted this way and that, filling glasses, telling jokes, laughing and puffing out his cheeks. How puckish he was, she thought, her Robin Goodfellow. And once again, she wondered what she was doing here, in such a strange place, without David or Adam. Monday. Bank Holiday. She feared and hated Mondays. Eleven twenty-five p.m. The insistent, the morbid numerology of the bereaved.

Rob reappeared, dressed as Dracula in flowing cloak and top-hat, wing-collared shirt, cravat, make-up which hollowed out his cheeks, and ghastly fangs, and she saw that, despite the fangs, the style suited him: he had an authentic early nineteenth-century Romantic look. David would have approved, she thought, but would have wanted the fangs to be dripping tomato ketchup blood.

Count Dracula was followed by a Caliban-like slave banging a tambourine and wearing Rob's smelly old Afghan coat, always described by him as "more yash than mac". This creature groped at girls and women in their path, declaiming, "Make way for Count Dracula. He needs his nightly dose of virgin's blood. Are you a virgin, dear?"

Later on Rob came up to Sarah and whispered, "Remember Marianne? My very first love – you know, cried when she came – the one I flaunted so shamelessly at my mother? Well, she's here. She's come back to live. Her marriage, too, has failed." He paused. "She's still got her wonderful red hair. She's down in the cellar now, with Pete." Rob laughed and she thought she caught more resentment than amusement in it.

100

"Doesn't waste much time in getting even, does our Pete."

And once he came and brushed her cheek with the knuckles of one hand.

She'd go and ring Mel to see how David was, and she'd ring the magazine once again. Some of the staff were working overtime to get out a special supplement and they'd said that by midnight tonight they'd have definite news of Colin. She came back from the telephone dazed with relief, and had another glass of wine. Colin was safe. She'd spoken to him. He'd been in a sleeper which hadn't been hit. It was miraculous. She laughed a bit and cried, and looked for Rob to tell him the news, but he was nowhere to be seen.

The glowering Caliban creature came lurching towards her and introduced himself as "Heathcliff" and started declaiming bits of poetry.

"What's that?" she asked, removing herself from the fumes of booze and Afghan coat which emanated from him, and looking round distractedly for Rob.

"*Othello*. Don't you recognise it?"

"Look, have you seen Rob? I've got to speak to him."

"No. I haven't," said Caliban, doggedly following her. "Pretend he's vanished and you have to make do with me."

He came round in front of her and suddenly knelt at her feet. She backed away from him into the nearest chair, but he struggled across to her, on his knees.

"Know what I'd like?" he asked. "I'd like to lie naked in bed with you, and talk. Just talk, that's all. That's the best, you know. The tops. Nothing sexual – " He took a swig of beer and spluttered it on her foot. "Well, it could be sexual, if you wanted. If you weren't *his* friend." He cocked a knowing eye at her. "I was at school with your Rob," he said, as if he could tell her a thing or two. "Well, I'll tell you what I always say to women. It always works. I say: I want to kiss the inside of your thigh. And I say: I'd like to touch your breasts, but I wouldn't touch the nipple. Not for a long, long time." He glanced slyly up at her. "You're passionate, aren't you? When you want to be. I can tell."

Rob was tired and grumpy and it was almost morning by the time the last of the revellers left and they'd cleared up and gone to bed. People had abused the house, the furniture, his hospitality, he complained. Glasses were broken, ash dropped on carpets, plates of half eaten food left on chairs to be sat upon. A friend of Sarah's who was in the district had dropped in and he'd taken an instant dislike to her. "Loud and brittle," he said, over and over. "I can't for the life of me see what the connection is with you."

"Be charitable," Sarah said. "She's getting divorced. It's knocked her off-balance."

"Does she have to be so shrill? And, by the way, the salmon was underdone, you know. Those big fish *must* be cooked right through."

"You warned me and warned me to keep it moist. I was terrified of *over*cooking it."

"I don't know which is worse," he said, withdrawing his arm from underneath her and rolling over to the far side of the bed as if to say "don't touch me, don't cuddle me, I don't even want to be a spoon tonight."

Careful not to touch him by so much as the inadvertent graze of a knee, she turned away from him and stared out into the wet and blurry darkness.

Would Colin's experience on the train make him consider the sanctity of his own life? Didn't a narrow escape make one's life seem more precious, somehow? Experiencing Adam's death had certainly made David's life and her own more precious to her. And more precarious, too. A gift, marked "fragile, handle with care", something you dared not waste, nor take for granted. She still hadn't told Rob that Colin was all right. Much he would care! There was nothing he cared about, she told herself bitterly, that wasn't trivial. Why should she feel rejected if such a person failed to make love to her?

Next morning Rob brought her a breakfast tray with coffee and brown toast and eggs laid by his own hens less than an hour before. "I'll drive you up to London," he said. "I have to go up anyway. I've one or two things to do."

"Emily, my friend from Los Angeles, is arriving this afternoon."

"What time?"

"About four o'clock."

"I'll have you home by then."

Fields lay tilted into sunlight, hedgerows hid glimpses of cut corn and poppies straggled under fences and into ditches, brightening the roadsides everywhere, but a gloomy pall of cloud obscured the sky as they drove into London and Sarah thought, as they crossed Oxford Street and saw the crowds milling up and down, that since Adam had died the summer sky had never been clear over London, and every day seemed more oppressive than the last.

It was not something she would have dared to say, for although there had been a severe drought, grass had turned brown, and trees had died, people would be bound to think that it was her oppressive sense of grief that made the lowering sky seem threatening. As it was, she allowed herself to say too many things that no one understood. You miss a person more as time goes by, not less. And the reason is simple: they've been away from you longer, that's all. Oh, I'm fine this week, she used to reassure her friends, most weeks for months on end. Last week I was bad – I admit I was bad last week – but I'm okay now, I promise. I won't even cry in public.

"This place looks like something out of Fritz Lang's nightmare, *Metropolis*," said Rob, catching a glimpse of the mass of shoppers seething under a neon and indigo sky. "It beats me how you can live here. And on the third floor, too! I'd feel much happier if you had your feet on the ground."

Emily and a small, stout boy of eleven or twelve were unloading piles of suitcases from a taxi in front of Sarah's door. "Oh, no. She's brought her son," said Sarah, in dismay.

"I'll see you later," said Rob, driving off.

Sarah greeted the jet-lagged but formidably well-dressed Emily, and, accompanied by Vincent ("Isn't he cute? How d'you like his little Cardin blazer? Isn't it

104

natty? We bought it in Paris") and a great deal of Gucci luggage, struggled up to Sarah's flat.

The new visitors seemed to take a long and wearing time to settle in. David did not find Vincent cute, and Vincent did not find David friendly.

"Why do elephants wear ripple-soled sand shoes?" David greeted his new guest, to be rewarded by a long, suspicious, four-eyed stare. "To give the ants a 50-50 chance, stupid." David turned haughtily into his room, meaning, "I'm not sharing with that moron. How could you do such an awful thing to me?" Besides which, Emily simply failed to understand how Sarah could have lived so long without adequate closet space or clothes hangers.

Later that evening, over what remained of the duty free Scotch Emily had brought with her, Sarah was subjected to a blow-by-blow account of Emily's life as a Born Again Woman. It seemed that, after her divorce from Vincent's father, Emily had joined a consciousness-raising group, and soon after that, had become President of a multi-million-dollar association dedicated to helping women regain their self-esteem after the batterings of divorce. The irony was that, in doing this vital and selfless work for the community, Emily had not only grown rich and famous and become a media person, she had actually Found Herself.

"I really think I might have remained a 'token woman' all my life," she said, pouring herself another whisky. "As it is, the movement has changed my life. Take this, for instance – " She waved the glass of whisky in front of Sarah. "I used to be an alcoholic. Can you believe it? Me? And then I joined AA and I was cured. Now I never touch the stuff. It's tomato juice all the way. Well, tonight, I admit, is different. I'm a little bit discombobulated, tonight.

"Eleven hours in a plane and the shock of yesterday's election results. Was it yesterday? Oh, haven't I told you what happened? It was total disaster. The committee failed to re-elect me. So I'm left with the major problem of what am I going to do with myself next year? I've had eleven hours at thirty-three thousand feet thinking about nothing else, and I tell you, Sarah, I still don't have a clue. See, I've gotten used to being an executive person now, with all the perks and the travel that goes with that. Y'know, no wonder I'm discombobulated. My future's just fizzled out.

"Vincent was really supportive on the trip. What that kid understands by now is quite unreal. And my man'll be supportive, too, though he didn't like it when I first became a feminist, no more than any of 'em do. Kept telling me I was being strident. But when it dawned on him that it was kind of the thing in our circles in L.A. and that it was fashionable to be supportive, he tried, he really tried. I don't know what he'll do when he hears they voted me out after all the work I've done. He'll be outraged. He'll probably want to fight it all the way. He's a lawyer and lawyers like to fight. Lawyers are very powerful in L.A."

Just then the doorbell rang and Rob arrived. This is a first-rate recipe for disaster, Sarah thought, as she introduced them: the English country squire and the American Born Again Woman President. It was not long before she was proved correct.

"Don't I get offered anything in this house?" Rob opened, prowling around the room straightening pictures, tweaking curtains, picking up cushions from the floor. I have prior claim on this territory, his behaviour announced to Emily, while Sarah disgraced herself in Emily's eyes by getting up guiltily from her chair and saying, "Of course you do, darling. What would you like?"

"I'd like to slip into a long, cool gin and tonic for starters," Rob said. "I'm not hungry. I had a curry with Giles."

Sarah mixed Rob's drink, adding lots of ice and stirred it with a swizzle stick liberated from the Algonquin Hotel, New York.

"No slice of fresh lemon or your favourite lime," she apologised. "Compared with yours, this establishment leaves a great deal to be desired."

Emily watched this exchange as if she could not believe her eyes or ears. "You're pandering to him, Sarah. I'm surprised at you. People don't behave like that anymore."

Rob wheeled round and confronted her. "They do round here," he said, standing with feet apart and chest puffed out. Emily ignored him and addressed herself to Sarah. "Behaviour like that tells a man that you think he's superior."

"Correct," said Rob. "We are. So you needn't bother to gang up on me." He looked at the intruder pityingly. "I'm a countryman," he said. "I've spent years studying the animal kingdom. Millions of years of natural evolution have made the male of the species stronger. Fact." He turned to Sarah and asked rhetorically, "Did your friend travel here on an aeroplane piloted by a woman?

107

Of course she didn't. Would you fly on a plane with a woman pilot?"

"Any minute now you're going to ask me where is the female Botticelli," said Sarah, getting ready to make an exit. "That is the point at which I always leave the party. I'm going to bed. Good night."

"That's right. Run away from the fight," said Rob.

"God help us," Emily said, as Sarah opened the door.

"She will," said Sarah.

Ten minutes later Rob came in, and stood glowering at her as she sat in bed.

"I've abandoned your friend," he said grimly, with a short, sharp laugh Sarah didn't like. "And since male company is so distasteful to you, I think I'll be on my way. It was nice knowing you."

"Rob! For Christ's sake!"

"You really meant what you said in there, didn't you?" he said coldly. "You really do think women are superior."

"That's racist talk," she said. "And I don't like it. Especially in my bedroom. Someone has to feel denigrated. Don't you know yet that everyone thinks their own tribe is superior, while secretly fearing the next tribe really is? I thought you understood." She tried to soft-pedal the disappointment in her voice, but saw him recoil from it all the same.

"I saw girls in London today who were making themselves look like men, trying to be like men. These feminists are a lot of lesbians. Women used to be such pretty things, well-dressed and appealing, with make-up and shiny hair."

"Emily doesn't look like a man."

"But she's trying to act like one."

"And what do you mean by 'things'?"

"You look quite different when you talk like this. Not like yourself at all."

"Wanting equal rights doesn't mean wanting to be the same," Sarah said desperately. "Haven't you thought this through? Equal but different. That's the essence of it. The Bantu don't want to be Eskimo but they both want human rights. Women don't want to be like men – why would that be such great shakes? Look what a mess your lot has made of the world."

Rob's face was pale and set with fury. "So you think it's time that women took over, is that it? And you'd do better."

"Don't be stupid, Rob."

"Don't call me stupid."

He paused and started towards her, and for a moment she thought he was going to hit her. "I feel betrayed. All the time I've known you, or thought I knew you, you've been secretly thinking all this stuff. I had no idea that all this rubbish was going on in your head. You've condescended to love me as an inferior. The cheek of it."

He stood poised for flight, his hand on the doorknob, his bum outlined dramatically against the dark of the hall behind him, and she thought how good his figure looked in the gear she'd recently bought for him.

"This is the worst shock I've had since all that time ago when Ange had her miscarriage and lost our baby."

"What on earth's that got to do with it?" Sarah asked, appalled.

"She didn't tell me till then that she'd had three abortions. Before she met me, of course. I felt betrayed then, too. She should have told me before I married her. I felt I'd been cheated. She'd kept a vital experience secret from me, and, as her future husband, she must have known that the state of her body concerned me. She was supposed to produce my heirs."

Sarah shook her head to try and clear her ears. Could she really be hearing these words at two a.m. of a summer's morning in the late twentieth century?

"And you, with all this feminist crap – you've hidden your true beliefs from me. You should have known that what's in your mind concerns me."

There was a pause while they looked at one another in disbelief.

"I'm leaving," he announced. The bedroom door shut behind him, and then the front door slammed. Sarah sat there in bed trying to absorb the shock.

"If you can leave over this," she told the empty room, "then go." She observed with surprise that she wasn't even shaking.

"If he can be that stupid," she said to Mel on the telephone, "how can I possibly care?"

"You can," said Mel.

"But I wasn't even shaking."

"No comment," said Mel.

"They're quite extraordinary," Sarah said. "There are

110

the ones, like Adam, who make all the right liberal noises, and seem concerned to show they are rational human beings, switched on to new ideas. But their gut reaction to women is the same as it's always been these last five thousand years. They clap their hands and expect you to bring their tea."

"Haven't you learned yet – there's very little link up between what they think and how they feel or behave. Most men are terrified of women, and the moment we become censorious, they identify us with their mothers and have to run away. Poor things – they're constantly rebelling and having to leave home."

"Then there are men like Rob who spout all kinds of reactionary rubbish, but are – oddly – easier to live with. On a daily basis they even seem prepared to do equal chores. In Rob's case because he feels he does them better, but even so . . ."

"It's unfortunate Emily was there. I expect he felt the two of you were ganging up on him," said Mel. "Making fun of some of his worst fears. They can't bear to be laughed at, men."

"And they think whenever two or more of us are gathered together, we laugh at them all the time."

"How on earth could they think such an awful thing?" asked Mel.

Rob rang her at noon next day, a small, penitent voice on the telephone.

"Well, I was punished, wasn't I? I ran into fog on the motorway and had to sleep cramped in the car. I've only

111

just got home." A pause and then he said, distinctly, "You've got to remember one thing, with me."

"Oh, yes," said Sarah. "What's that?"

Rob took a deep breath, then expelled the words with force. "The drive away from the mother," he said, and cut the telephone cord between them.

7

Sarah lay back in the sports car and stretched luxuriously. The newly harvested Suffolk cornfields stretched, too, on either side of them, golden in the slanting, mellow sunlight of late afternoon. Poppies and a few late cornflowers showed at the cornfields' edges, and straggled through the hedgerows.

"This car's the ideal level for seeing lots of sky," Sarah said, watching haystacks fly past, and the dark golden stooks, like rolls of carpet waiting to be laid, and the long, curved furrows rolling on and on to the horizon, interrupted only by the occasional square church tower, stolidly standing in the shade of its own large tree.

"And for feeling lots of thigh," said Keith, taking his left hand from the steering wheel and putting it just above her knee. Sarah laughed and stretched her arms along the back of his seat. Gosh, he was nice, Keith. So much nicer than she'd thought all those years she'd worked with him and he'd taken his blue pencil to her copy.

"I have to get out of town," she told him one day at the office. "First anniversary of the dreadful day coming up. I need to go somewhere. I'll have to work too hard to think of it all the time. Can't you send me on a special assignment, Keith? I'm desperate."

"I'm going to Ipswich for an early morning meeting with the printers," he'd said. "Staying in Suffolk overnight. Come with me, if you like. The drive'll do you good. I can't promise to distract you from the grislies, though."

"I wish they still had the old-fashioned corn stooks," she said, now. "The biblical ones that looked like little wigwams." She was thinking how much easier it was to be with Keith than she'd imagined. Perhaps it was possible to escape, after all, if one kept the tone of things light and relaxed, like this, and made sure that what you weren't seeking was replacement.

"They're cutting down two of my plane trees in the square," she told him. "My beautiful planes. They're under preservation, you know. The noise, the whine of the saws is dreadful. They say they've got rot, just those two, but they *look* absolutely fine."

Keith switched Vivaldi off. "Can't hear at this speed," he said.

"It was another reason I had to get away – to avoid the noise and seeing the branches fall. It's the end of something, like – "

"The sound of the axes in the cherry trees. Like *The Cherry Orchard*."

He asked her about David, and they talked about his two children.

"Would you like to hear my son's new non-robot joke?" she asked him. "What's the difference between a railway porter, a schoolteacher and a pot of glue?"

Keith put on a music-hall comedian voice. "I don't know. What *is* the difference between a railway porter, a schoolteacher and a pot of glue?"

"A railway porter minds trains, and a teacher trains minds."

"Oy – what about the pot of glue?"

114

"Ah, Mum, that's where you get stuck."

They crunched up a gravel driveway and stopped in front of a large stone house. There were several cars in the car park, and several more in the drive.

"Good thing I booked," said Keith.

An air of excitement hung about inside, transforming the placid faces of bell-boys and receptionists and lending the dim floral carpets and the corridors smelling of beef a certain mystery. Even the moth-eaten stags looking down from the walls seemed to know a thing or two.

"What's the buzz?" asked Keith of the bartender.

"Harvest festival, guv. Big dance tonight."

"I don't believe it," said Keith into Sarah's ear as he whirled her round the dance floor. "Is this really us?"

Around them danced solid Suffolk farming folk, earnestly enjoying an evening off. They ate all the courses, between dances, including trifle, and discovered with some surprise they could do the old-fashioned steps quite well together.

"Any minute now I'm going to have to stop all this relaxing and interview you," Sarah told him. "I'm just giving you due warning. You can't moan and groan about my series being all about women, unless you're prepared to give me some masculine points of view."

Keith grimaced. "I know those editor types," he said. "The more grisly and traumatic the confessions you get, the better the bastards like it."

Outside the tall windows hung a huge, yellow harvest moon, watching over shorn fields, silvering what was gold so recently, and leaving a decent shadow at the churchyard's edges, where the new graves were dug.

She shivered, and they went upstairs. He had taken adjoining rooms, but decided to give her a nightcap, first, in his. It contained an enormous Victorian mahogany wardrobe smelling of mothballs with a cracked mirror and two bent wire hangers inside it, and a great big lumpy bed. Keith found a Gideon Bible in the bedside drawer, stripped himself naked, without revealing himself to her, got into bed and began to read to her from the Song of Songs.

"How beautiful are thy feet with shoes, O Prince's daughter, The joints of thy thighs are like jewels, The work of the hands of a cunning workman, Thy navel is like a round goblet which wanteth not liquor, Thy belly is like an heap of wheat set about with lilies. Thy two breasts are like two young roes that are twins . . ."

Sarah sat on the bed beside him and with his Bible-free hand he stroked her two young roes through the thin silk of her blouse.

"How fair and pleasant art thou, O love, for delights."

Suddenly Keith began to shake with laughter. "Hark at this, Sarah. 'Christ setteth forth the graces of the Church,'" he read. "'He sheweth His love to her. The Church prayeth to be made fit for His presence.' Believe that and you'll believe anything."

116

Sarah seized the book from him, and read:

"My Beloved put in his hand by the hole of the door
and my bowels were moved for him."

Keith rocked the bed with laughter.

"I rose up to open to my Beloved, and my hands
dropped with Myrrh, and my fingers with sweet
smelling myrrh, upon the handles of the lock. I
opened to my Beloved but my Beloved had with-
drawn himself and was gone."

Keith drew Sarah towards him and began kissing her
hair and her neck underneath her hair.

"My soul failed when he spake;" she read. "I
sought him but I could not find him; I called him
but he gave me no answer."

"Oh, God!" said Sarah, putting down the book. She
began to cry, and Keith took the Bible from her and
continued:

"Thou hast ravished my heart, my sister, my
spouse . . . How much better is thy love than wine,
and the smell of thine ointments than all spices!

"I know. Don't cry. I shouldn't have brought you
here at harvest festival. It's all the influence of that
opulent pregnant-bellied moon.

"Thy lips drop as the honeycomb, honey and milk
are under thy tongue . . ."

Keith stopped reading for a moment to kiss Sarah, his tongue tracing her lips, circling her tongue. Who could have imagined he would kiss so beautifully?

"Thy plants are an orchard with pleasant fruits . . .
Let my Beloved come into his garden and eat his pleasant fruits."

She began to cry in earnest.

"A garden enclosed is my sister, my spouse, a spring shut up, a fountain sealed."

"And now," he said, "the fountain overflows," for it seemed that all the kisses in the world were not enough, tonight, to stop her tears.

"You're so restless," said Mel, restlessly sliding up and down the newly scrubbed, stripped, sanded and polished playroom floor, with rags serving as dusters under her feet, and orchestrating the movements of half a dozen children similarly employed. "You've hardly got back from one place when you're off to another, and now you tell me you're taking your ma-in-law on a pilgrimage to the Holy Land! I've never heard anything like it."

Sarah watched her friend with the usual mixture of irony, amusement and affection. Mel had quarrelled with Chris over her project to turn the two ground floor rooms into an extended playroom by knocking down a wall or two, getting rid of most of the furniture and all the carpets and laying bare the floorboards. Chris had not shared her vision, Mel complained, had not seemed keen to help her, had not "pulled his weight". She had told him to go, but he hadn't realised how serious she was, and pending his departure, Mel had moved into the spare room to sleep. Then she had set about punishing herself by doing every bit of the work, alone, in the hardest, most painstaking way, even scrubbing the floor on her hands and knees with an old-fashioned scrubbing brush, soap and pail.

"You see," she showed Sarah, waving her hands triumphantly as she demonstrated to the children how to skate on the dusters without losing them, or tripping over. "My fingers are worked to the bone, as our mothers and grandmothers used to say." And indeed they were red, the knuckles skinned raw, the flesh puffy in the space above the torn cuticles and broken nails. But Mel's dancer's movements, as she whirled round the room, and froze the children into statues when the music stopped, were as graceful as a figure on the bonnet of an early motorcar, signifying speed, flight, motion – or restlessness.

"That's all right. I think you're off your rocker, too," Sarah said. "If you weren't, would I allow your constant flow of criticism?"

"We're both of us teetering on the verge of sanity, as Wyndham Lewis is supposed to have said of Boswell."

Mel executed an ambitious pirouette, David stepped on her duster and they both crashed to the ground. Giggling and shrieking the other children fell in a delighted heap on top of them.

★

"It's absolutely true," Sarah admitted later, over coffee. "I'm doing as much travelling now as Adam ever did. One of my more charming colleagues told me I was like a chicken running round after it had lost its head."

"Ugh," said Mel, screwing her eyes up tight against the gruesome image, and shuddering.

"But it's apt," said Sarah. "The body goes on working."

The dreadful tape, Adam's body jerking, left right left, played once more on the screen in her head, preyed once again on her darkened mind.

"You're trying to escape, I suppose," Mel said, clasping her poor, frayed hands round the chipped enamel mug for warmth, glad, for once, of the strength in her bitter, tooth-curling coffee.

"I'm trying to be Adam, don't you see? Travelling like he did. Doing what he did. Saying what he said. Telling his old jokes and laughing at them. I freaked out some old mates of his the other day by saying, just as they were tucking in, 'Let's eat this lobster for Adam. He'd adore it!' They completely lost their appetites, poor things." She gave a snort of laughter. "I'm trying to be both of us, live for both of us, keep it all going."

"Wouldn't it be better if you just tried to be yourself?" said Mel.

"Ouch! Bullseye!" said Sarah. And then, after a pause, "It's funny, isn't it? I go into every new situation, a foreign country, a weekend in a country house, somebody else's lifestyle, thinking maybe this is it, this is how I should live, I should bring David here and we could set up home and start a new life and perhaps we'd be happy. I arrive on the Friday and everything seems idyllic, my hosts calm and smiling in their enchanted setting, the house running smoothly, a delicious dinner appearing effortlessly. And by Sunday lunchtime every member of the household has confessed to an advanced state of trauma. The wife's upstairs packing to leave on Monday morning, Nanny's in the kitchen taking valium, and the husband, who was on the wagon, has found a secret store of Scotch.

"The neighbours have discovered just how implicated their partners were, the teenagers are locked in the play-room trying out dangerous substances, and the dog has been shot for chasing a nearby farmer's sheep. It is then that I realise this is not the life I want for me and David and I head home to my lonely mausoleum of a flat. But I never learn the lesson. I set out hopefully each time."

"Anything to avoid facing what you have to face," said Mel gently. "That your new status is widowhood. That you have to remake your life as a woman facing society alone. It's hard. But whatever happens to you in the future, whatever relationships you may make, you cannot begin to live again until you accept that fact."

Sarah stared at Mel, amazed. "But that would mean abandoning Adam. Accepting that he's really dead."

"Exactly," said Mel, looking back at her, unblinking.

Sarah walked home across the park with David. The sky was low and heavy with humidity so that veils of mist hung in the air and the branches of trees seemed weighted down with their burden of dusty, dark green leaves, their weariness proclaiming the end of summer. Familiar skylines were misted over, the clammy air tasted of metal, the colours were all shades of steel: the clouds swirling dull as lead, the lake glimmering like polished aluminium. The birds were restless, as in a false spring, exotic foreign geese ruffling the surface of the water with their flapping and cackling and noisy quarrelling. Ducks flew up in threes as they do on countless sitting room walls across the country, deckchairs were everywhere arranged in twos: would she, Sarah, ever learn to be one, to be herself, alone?

"Find the essential woman," urged the magazines she worked for, patiently, month after month, year after year. "Learn to be yourself. Discover who you are. Live your own life."

Large charcoal-grey pieces of plane tree bark lay curled like modern sculptures on the grass, crisp, dry and full of holes, waiting for David to jump on them. Sarah joined in the game: the bark made the most agreeable noise as one crunched it underfoot. They passed a bank of phlox and larkspur and delphiniums, bright dahlias and bronze and yellow helium. In a long, hot summer, even herbaceous borders planted with annuals had a second flowering, but Sarah would rather enter the safety of a second childhood than risk the stirrings of even the falsest of false springs.

"Hey, Mum, I forgot to ask you. Why wouldn't the skeleton come out of the cupboard?"

"I don't know, David. Why wouldn't the skeleton come out of the cupboard?"

"Because it didn't have the guts."

Around the Serpentine a stately parade was taking place, an early evening *paseo* of elegance and distinctive ethnic chic. Groups of voluminously black-garbed women passed like dangerous birds in beaky metallic masks; gaggles of glamorous over-groomed Arab girls glowing in costly, brightly patterned silks cut in the latest, most outlandish styles, followed by packs of female servants whose misshapen bodies, pock-marked complexions and downcast eyes contrasted oddly with the silken brilliance of their mistresses' last season's cast-offs.

There were Japanese gentlemen taking group photographs and Indian ladies sauntering in gold and silver saris; there were flocks of white robed Arab sheikhs feeding the ducks and Nigerian giants in bright red hats and golden braid, skins plump and polished as ripe black end-of-season plums. Sarah wondered why the herbaceous borders bothered. They couldn't compete at all.

David came up to her, presented his back, and asked her, in his best robot voice, to wind him up. She did so, and he marched off, moving his limbs mechanically and chanting mechanical slogans to himself. Watching him in his trendy tracksuit and running shoes Sarah walked into a cloud of midges hanging in the air at face level by the water's edge, and beat them off savagely, while trying to control a ridiculous feeling of panic. They were out to get her. They weren't ordinary English midges, they were dirty, disease ridden flies. Who knew where they had been or what horrible infections they could carry? Malevolent forces were at work: they had stricken Adam down, and now they were out to get her and David. And the worst thing was they lay in wait for you, everywhere.

"Eliminate-Enemy-Armies. Destroy. Annihilate," croaked David, marching unperturbed round Sarah. "Insect-Menace-Located-And-Destroyed," he reported to headquarters, then switching to his normal voice said, "Come on, Mummy, they're only gnats." He pushed her in front of him at the point of a long stick he'd found in the grass and marched her off.

As Sarah's heartbeat slowed to normal, she started her exotic-people-watching again. What do they make of our romantic landscape, so damp, so leafy, so mysterious? What do they make of all this ambiguity, veil upon misty veil – our scenery, our language and our manners? Does it change their lives for ever, they who were born under the remorseless clarity of desert skies? For they, in their turn, were certainly changing London, that great arterial river of life forever absorbing new components into its vital bloodstream, moving onwards, flowing, enriching itself, surviving.

And what flows in me, she thought, but tears and endless grief? I'm locked into the past, a clock stopped at the awful moment, incapable of change. And if you don't change, you die. London flows, David grows, and I stagnate, talking only of the past, laughing only at old jokes, keeping everything as it was. I'm like Adam's wristwatch, which stopped on the third day after his death, at twenty past three in the afternoon: the day and the time they had put him into the ground. Oh, the sound of those heavy clods of earth falling on the wooden box. The worst sound in the world. Sarah put her hands over her ears. *To think they should lay him in the cold ground.* How I'd love to go mad. The relief of it. The blessed release. To scream and scream and not care if anybody heard, to tear my hair, to sob with that violence that stretches the mouth until it tears, and distorts the face for weeks. Only not to have to take responsibility.

But these days, Ophelia, they don't leave you alone, picking herbs, they take you in, and lay you out as if you, too, were a corpse. They inject you full of tranquillisers. They give you shocks and pills. And after two weeks, when the pain is suppressed instead of exorcised, they shove you out into the world again, less able to cope and more confused than ever. No, I'll hang on to my sanity, if that's what it is, to my balance, though the cost is very high.

And sometimes I'm damn sure that I'm not sane.

Since Adam had died she had not moved one item of furniture in the house, or changed one thing, and the whole place was beginning to look as unnatural as a museum. Out of date, she thought suddenly, shocked. And what of the furniture of her mind? The details of his jokes she told so often belonged already to another era, to the fads and fashions and jargon of an earlier time. What would Adam say if he knew that David had grown so tall, or had done this and said that? What would he think of inflation, of that new building over there, the weather, the political situation, the future of the BBC? Sarah went about boasting, "I always know what Adam thinks about everything," and she boasted in the present tense. But the world went on without him and how could she know what he would think about the new?

They came home and went straight into the kitchen where Sarah put the kettle on for coffee and prepared toasted sandwiches for David, these being the only food he would eat since they had acquired their toasted-sandwich machine last week.

"Look, Mummy, there's a drip coming from the ceiling." Sarah looked. A heavy bulge had appeared in the middle of the kitchen ceiling and the drip was issuing from it, under pressure. A small puddle was gathering on the kitchen floor. Sarah switched off the electrical appliances, grabbed David and pulled him out of the door.

"I have to go upstairs and see what's causing it," she said, sitting him down in front of the TV set and thinking that she'd always known the quarrels of the divorcing couple in the flat upstairs would cause some problems. "I'll have to make some holes in the ceiling to let the water out, so the whole thing doesn't fall on us."

As she said this, there was an almighty crash, a terrifying cracking, shattering, tearing noise, like a bomb exploding. They clung to one another till the crashing stopped, then David broke loose and went to look. "Oh, Mummy. The whole ceiling's fallen down," he said excitedly. "There's water and gungy stuff all over everywhere and funny dust – " he began to cough, " – so thick I can hardly see."

"Come back in here," said Sarah. "Don't breathe it in." She covered her face with her hands. "I don't want to look," she said. "I bet it looks worse than old newsreels of the Blitz. And I bet all our china's shattered."

Sarah called the neighbours, the caretaker, the emergency plumbers and the insurance company. For the next few days they had breakfast and supper at McDonald's and she spent most of the time in between filling in insurance forms, calling decorators and supervising a firm of emergency cleaners manned by strapping Home-Counties debutantes and winsomely dubbed Dynamic Dusters.

"Scrubbers, I'd call it," said Mel sourly. She had popped in to survey the mess and was secretly hankering after scrubbing the place herself. "We thought of 'Cinderellas'," said one boyish debutante called George (for Georgina), "but Mummy thought it was a trifle twee."

"And Henry positively threw up," said Jocelyn.

"Who's Henry?" asked Mel.

"Her boyfriend," said Jocelyn.

"No, he's not," said George smugly. "He's my fiancé."

"Oh, I see," said Mel. "Or should I say 'Hooray'?"

"The inside of every single cupboard is full of water and insulating gunge," Sarah said, as they sat in the comparatively dust free air of the park. "It'll take several scrubbings, and complete redecoration before the place seems really clean again. And before I can do any of that, they have to fix the ceiling."

"And let it dry," said Mel. "What colours will you choose? Now's your chance to re-plan, you know. You could have a new kitchen on insurance if you play it right."

"Well, I thought I'd have cornflower blue and deep terracotta," said Sarah, "and maybe some pine panelling too. But I feel so odd about it. No one's contradicted me. I keep waiting for Adam to say 'Ugh' and tell me to have it all done in white."

"You've been forced to change," said Mel, "and still you feel guilty. Whatever will we do with you?"

"I'm imposing my will on the place," said Sarah. "Once it was ours. If I take the decisions, it will be mine alone. God, I'm so fed up with having to cope alone. What a relief it would be to be able to share these household disasters. If Adam had been here – "

"He'd have got the dubbing theatre booked for twenty-four hours – and we all know what that costs – and he'd say – "

"Ring the plumbers, darling. Ring the insurance company. Sort it out. Sorry, I must dash." She paused. "Or he'd be in Africa."

They looked at one another and laughed.

"Why do we persist in thinking that life is not coped with alone, in or out of marriage? Why do we try so hard to live our lives through other people, twisting ourselves through every kind of hoop to avoid a life of our own?"

"Oh, females are brought up to think of others first."

"Rubbish," said Mel.

"I suppose we think it's easier, but it isn't, it's harder, actually."

"They're equally hard," said Mel, "but one's right and the other wrong."

Sarah stared at her in surprise. "You don't often use those words," she said.

David rushed up to where the two women sat and threw himself, face down, on to the grass, his whole body shaking. "Mummy, Mummy," he sobbed. "I saw Daddy. He was in the car, down by the Serpentine. It was our old red car, you know, the convertible. I ran towards him but he didn't see me. He just drove off."

He pounded the grass with his fists. "You see, Mummy, it isn't true. I told you it wasn't true. He isn't dead at all. He lives in another part of London." He put his head down and his tears ran over the backs of his tightly clenched hands. "Doesn't he love us anymore? Doesn't he want to see us?"

8

The bus smelled of tin and warm leatherette and stale sandwiches, its wheels jerking in and out of holes as it raced and rattled its way in darkness along what seemed to Sarah the whole of the length of the land of Israel. Outside and somewhere to the left, behind eucalyptus and scrubby pine, lay that long, straight, windy coast-line dismissed by Lawrence Lady Bracknell Durrell as the Mediterranean's wrong side. Sarah glanced across at Adela, who, now there were very few passengers left in the bus, had seated herself across the aisle, bolt upright, her forearms tense, both hands gripping the rail in front of her. She had tied a chiffon scarf over the famous upswept blonde hairdo, and her heavy-lidded blue eyes stared straight ahead with the bemused expression of a child, while her chin and her lower lip jutted forward, ready to defy or defend.

"You must be completely mad," said Adam's voice in Sarah's ear. "I hope you aren't telling yourself you're doing this for me. A pilgrimage? Pah! Two weeks in a hot little Middle Eastern country with my mother would drive anybody round the twist! It's certainly not something I'd ever do myself. Well, rather you than me! You haven't thought this through. As usual. You haven't considered what it would mean to lug a woman seventy-seven years old halfway across the world, a woman who never travels, who hates to travel. And then when she gets off the plane at Lod you rattle her poor old bones across the wilderness all the way to Galilee. Okay, she'd never find out if Israel had developed into the Promised Land. She'd never get very far from the Finchley Road. So what?"

The bus jerked to a stop. Sarah helped Adela off and checked their luggage as it was set down beside them. The bus – the last sign of life visible in a dark and empty landscape – disappeared. They were two women alone on the shores of Galilee, or so Sarah supposed. The only thing she was sure of was that they were alone. Fighting off a feeling of panic, Sarah peered into the blackness around them, but all she could see was a plank covering a muddy hole, and beyond the plank, some scaffolding. They were on a building site.

"Where are we?" quavered Adela. Sarah gazed up at the stars for inspiration, but though they shone with unaccustomed brilliance they were in unaccustomed places and she could not read them. They seemed just as far away as they would from any unholy land. Behind the scaffolding she glimpsed some dim but ordinary, non-celestial light.

"We shall have to walk the plank," she said.

"You go," said Adela faintly. "I'll wait here."

Sarah glanced around for thieves or gangsters, but nothing stirred. There was no sound at all, no sense of being near a mass of water, but then, of course, the "sea" of Galilee was not a sea at all, it was a lake, Tiberias, or Kinneret (the Harp), and subject to no tides nor waves nor scent of ozone.

"Stay with the luggage, then. I won't be a moment." She picked her way across the plank in the general direction of the light.

131

A dimly lit marble hall lay tucked at an angle behind a barrier of sepia glass doors. Sarah had never been so glad in her life to see the lobby of a hotel. She fetched Adela, and a bell-boy fetched the cases. But the nightmare wasn't over.

"We have no rooms for you in the name of this travel agency," an impassive woman behind the desk informed her. She checked a list of names. "Let me see. We have no rooms for you in your names, either."

"There must be some mistake," said Sarah. "Look, ring this number here, the agency's head office in Tel Aviv. I'm sure they will confirm our booking. We can call London if you like. I'll pay." The very taste of "London" on her tongue made her long to weep.

"Madam, it's two a.m.," the woman said. "Come. I'll give you a room together for tonight, and tomorrow we'll sort it out."

They fell into their beds without discussion, and though the room was stifling and Sarah couldn't open a window or work the air-conditioning, and wasn't even sure she'd locked the door, Adela fell sound asleep. Which was just as well, for at five a.m. the pneumatic drills began outside their window.

Light. It filled every corner, searched every pore. There was no use hiding from it. You could pull the rough weave curtains across the planes of invisible window glass but that light, that special light would seep into your very soul and search out each sin and wrinkle cowering there. The mornings were still with light, a perfect stillness. In the early morning there was haze, and then there was clarity, the stupefying clarity of noon. And then there was haze again. The water lapped against huge, round boulders, sucking and pulling at clusters of smaller stones which formed miniature sandy coves. There were biblical bulrushes, and birds. Men fished in the formal wintry garb of Hassidic Jews, their broad-brimmed eighteenth-century hats and black silk coats dusty with piety. A boy water-skied in a joyous circle on this water where a man once walked.

A sudden commotion in the stillness. An orthodox student of the Talmud from the Yeshivah on the right, dressed in black knickerbockers, his sidecurls flying, chased two caftanned Arab boys along the waterfront. What had they done? The hunter and the hunted ran swift as the waterfowl that skimmed the surface of the lake, past mosque and school and modern hotel and ancient inn, the boat and the boathouse, the episcopalian church, the wobbly jetty of bleached and rotting wood. And disappeared. Each ethnic and religious group seeking its own truth, preaching its own vision, teaching The Only Vision. Sarah and Adela, two widows recently bereaved, two women washed up on the wilder shores of grief, talked, cried and quarrelled.

"You are wrong, Sarah. You don't know what you're saying. I lived through it. I should know. The Germans were not the worst. The Germans hated us because we were Poles, but the Poles hated us because we were Jews."

Too much clarity can be confusing.

The world was nothing but a luminous bowl of light where lake and sky became each other constantly.

Anything could happen in this place, even the past could be illuminated. What was Sarah seeking on this pilgrimage, she with her baggage of half baked multi-ethnic hopes and fears? A blinding flash on the road to Tiberias? A High Priest to tell her how she should live without Adam? A guru to explain that she had no option now but to be herself? She'd shirked responsibility for that self in the sacred name of marriage. Surely God's wrath would petrify her, turn her, like Lot's poor wife, into a pillar of salt? For we must be ourselves, *per se*, not by default, not by most grievous default. Every person a rounded self, whole and entire, seeking love but not completion. Is this the Way and the Life?

Adela knew what she was seeking, here in Israel. Are you my child? she would ask every handsome young soldier guarding a church, a mosque, a newly excavated Roman temple, the mosaic floor of a second-century synagogue or palace. Are you my child? A very young girl from Uruguay encountered on the waterfront regarded Adela with dark and ardent eyes. "I have heard the voice of Jesus," she told them. "He was speaking to me, alone. Angelica, he said, you must go to the Holy Land, my land, where I was born. And so I came here. And here I am." She read from the Bible, with eyes upturned, like one of those sickly madonnas by Guido Reni. On and on, she read, in an accent full of clotted Spanish gutturals, until the sky darkened and the empty churches closed.

"She is not my child," Adela concluded sadly.

A sudden glimpse of David marching along by a lake less burdened with history flashed into Sarah's mind, accompanied by a pang of homesickness. She missed *her* child. To think she had felt ethnic confusion by the Serpentine, and believed she'd find clarification under hot, Middle Eastern skies!

"I told you," said Adam's voice, again. "My mother had no idea there were Christians or Arabs living here at all. She thought that Israel was an extension of Golders Green Road in the days before the Raj of Belsize Pakistan."

"When I visited Tel Aviv with my husband, in the early days of the State, things were very different," the old woman said, as if she, too, had heard Adam speak. "Everywhere we encountered Jews like ourselves from Eastern Europe who had never had a country of their own. We were all of us in a state of patriotic fervour. I remember we met an elderly man who was sweeping the street in front of our hotel. A most distinguished-looking grey-haired man, he reminded me of Ben Gurion. He spoke to us in an excellent High German – a Professor of Languages from Romania. 'So what is a Professor doing sweeping the streets?' asked Jacob. You know what the Romanian answered him? 'In my own house I shouldn't sweep the floor?'"

But Sarah really got into trouble with Adela when she started to make friends with Richard, a tall, European-looking boy who spoke good English and had a pleasant manner. Richard came from a nearby Arab village, his family had lived in Palestine and had been Christians, too, for ever. He had been teaching politics and history at a local school and told them proudly he had been dismissed, implying that this had been because his views were so subversive. Meanwhile, he worked as a porter at their hotel.

Richard took Sarah and Adela on a boat ride across the lake where they were shown a Kibbutz on the other side. He had brought Sarah the strangest of gifts, a smooth, round pebble he'd inscribed very carefully with her name in Hebrew letters. He made her throw it into the water from the boat, and together they watched it sink. He didn't explain to Sarah what this ceremonious gesture meant, but the idea of a pebble with her name upon it lying at the bottom of this historic lake until the trumpets sounded on judgement day was more than a little disturbing to her.

There had been a time, at the height of the grief and incomprehension, when Sarah had felt she was being forced to eat a large stone. She'd try to soften it with her lips, break it with her teeth, melt it with her tongue, but the stone refused to be broken down in any way, and try as she might, she could not accept it into her mouth or absorb it into her body. For the stone was unpalatable; inimical to human touch. And that cold, wet, smoothly oval stone, resistant to its solid, granite core, resembled Richard's pebble.

A darkly bronzed boy in khaki shorts drove the boat faster than he should, and lectured Sarah, his fierce blue eyes scanning her as if she were his horizon. "How can you trust that fellow? He's a Palestinian. They're all the same. Besides, he smuggles dope."

The next day Richard invited them to visit his family. He'd told his parents of the two nice English ladies and they'd invited them to their home to eat with them.

Richard had borrowed a car to drive them to the place, which was on their way back from the sacred hill town of Safed Sarah wanted so much to see. The rocky countryside smelled of wild thyme and flickered with

136

butterflies. The village had narrow mud streets and silent houses with blind walls, like sleeping eyes. There were donkeys and shrouded women, courtyards, a boy by a rusty pump, a toothless man who stared. Richard's family, his mother, father, brother, spoke a little English and behaved as if they were honoured by the visitors, which Sarah found embarrassing: they were there under false, or at least misleading, colours. Richard's father had been a policeman during the British Mandate and naturally thought that all English ladies must be Christians.

A sentimental figurine they had brought as a present was set, with exclamations of the politest pleasure, in a curious ledge in the door to the only room, where it could be easily admired. Sarah had wanted to bring Richard's mother flowers, but he had led her firmly to the rows of shiny porcelain figures lining the tourist shops and chosen an expensive crinolined girl complete with dog.

A meal of chicken and rice and yoghourt and pitta bread was served, the family deftly scooping their food from communal bowls with pieces of bread. After some moments, Richard's mother noticed Adela's awkwardness, and tin spoons and forks were produced without comment for her and Sarah.

Richard's brother was a dentist, and was to have married a Jewish ballerina, but the engagement had been broken off; he ate his meal hurriedly and asked if he might leave the table to get some sleep – he was working night shifts at the hospital. Through an open arch they could see him stretched out on an iron bed, his shoulders gleaming in dark contrast to his clean white vest.

There was a lemon tree in the courtyard on which hung many lemons, but they were bitter ones, it seemed, and not for culinary use. The olive tree in the courtyard, and the old olive press, provided a more fruitful topic for discussion, and Richard produced some olive oil for Sarah, in an old Johnny Walker bottle, the label glistening transparently. He wrapped it in a piece of an Arab newspaper which seemed to be mostly comic strips, in case she got oil on her pale pink linen dress.

"You're a traitor," Adela said, later, back in their hotel. Sarah had taken care to book separate rooms; she had to have her privacy, she knew. But Adela had found she could open, and keep wedged open, their communicating door, and said she couldn't sleep if it was shut. Sarah's revenge was to put the radio on late at night and do her dancing exercises to the loudest pop music she could find. She always felt full of energy when others went to sleep.

One night she sat on the floor surrounded by bits of paper and did a mock-up for the "Biblical" issue of a woman's magazine, complete with a knitting pattern for Joseph's coat of many colours, and a recipe for a "mess of pottage" which would not lose the cook her birthright.

"Traitor," Adela said again, rolling the rrs impressively. "If I'd known they were Arabs, do you think I'd have gone there and eaten in their house?"

Sarah looked at her mother-in-law with disgust. At that moment there was nothing about the old woman she did not loathe, even the cloying perfume she always wore, mixed with old-woman smell. The incongruities she usually enjoyed seemed ludicrous today, to say the least: the childish, knock-kneed way Adela stood (Adam had stood in exactly the same, annoying way), the aged eagle face and the obdurate Roman head set so absurdly atop her still voluptuous body. Oh, the curious, childlike bodies of the old! Adela had smooth young skin and vulnerable, full breasts with surprisingly long, still rosy, nipples. She had narrow shoulders and wide hips – in short, her body was still fuckable. But then there was the matter of teeth and hair. Her piled-up hair was swathed in a chiffon scarf for bed and the scarf always slipped low down across her brow making her look like a helmeted warrior in one of those large heroic canvases depicting Victory. And as for the teeth, like her famous namesake, her grandmother Adela, whom she had mocked so mercilessly as a child, Adela took them out each night to sleep – and there it was, a hag's face topping the large, soft, childish body – a cruel joke, a trick played by the silent passing of the years. The passive years. For what I am looking at, thought Sarah, fear replacing the disgust, is a body grown old without ever growing up. Adela had been a daughter, had "dwindled into a wife", had swelled, that once, into a mother. She had never been herself.

Sarah walked out of town with Richard, after dark. They left the churches, the synagogues, the religious colleges behind. They left the ancient Jewish and Roman towns of Tiberias and then the fairground and the straggle of gypsy caravans at the edge of it. The noise and the tinkling music of the fairground faded as they walked, and their footsteps on beaten mud made little sound. Richard wanted to show her the new town which was growing, higgledy piggledy, on the back of the tourist trade, and he wanted to show her his lodgings and his room. Sarah knew she was mad: she would be doped or raped, but curiosity led her on. That and the need to rebel against Adela.

He led her into an ordinary wooden frame house which smelled inside of incense and stale curry. There was no one else at home. His room was a simple student room, no furniture, rush matting on the floor and posters on the wall. He lit a candle in a saucer on the floor and sat cross-legged on his sleeping mat, beckoning to Sarah to sit down, too. "You fool!" she told herself, and yet she sat, and they looked at each other, silently. Then Richard gently bent towards her and because she did not want to kiss him, she took his head in her hands, her fingers touching his short, tight curls. She almost recoiled in shock: his hair felt coarse as wire wool, not like hair at all, or not like any hair she'd ever touched. But why did she feel so violently disturbed, as if she'd just discovered he was an alien from outer space and they'd forgotten to give him human ears? She held his head as steadily as she could for a moment or two, though she could not make her fingers caress the wiriness, then she removed her hands and got slowly to her feet.

"Richard," she said, looking down at him from a safe height. "I am glad I saw your pad. It's very nice. But I think I had better get back now. You know how the old lady is, she'll worry about me if I'm late. The other night she got dressed after she'd gone to bed and was pacing about in the foyer until I came home."

Richard stood up and without a word, escorted her back to the hotel on the waterfront.

"She thinks, now, that we were twins, Adam and I," Sarah told Richard, gabbling in relief. "She's told herself that she had a boy and a girl and only the girl survived. She wants to believe, you see, that I'm really her child."

Early next day Sarah and Adela set off for Jerusalem through the wilderness. They followed the dry Jordan riverbed, stopping at primitive desert pull-ups for petrol and coffee and lavatories. At Jericho they turned up and into the echoing hills, where nothing but legend grew and a few skinny mountain sheep tried to graze on the prickly grey herbs which gave off a powdery smell that hung in the thin, keen air.

"The driver's an Arab, isn't he?" Adela asked. "I expect you got him on recommendation from Richard, your great friend. You're a fool, Sarah. You trust everyone and only a fool or a child or an idiot does that. Do you realise we could be killed? We could be mugged, or raped, or stoned to death on this road, with no one to protect us. The papers are full of such incidents." She turned her face away and gazed out at the pages of Bible flying past. Sarah kept quiet for once. Adela was voicing her worst fears.

The driver pulled the car to a shuddering stop at the top of a hill and gestured for them to get out, waving his hands about excitedly. Adela shrugged and sat where she was.

"He's run out of petrol," she said. "I expect we'll be stuck here till we rot and the sun bleaches us, too, to dry white bones."

"I suck her the bones!" Adela had said once, to Mel, just after Adam's funeral. And as Mel recoiled, she added quietly, "Yes, I love her so much, my Sarah, I finish whatever she leaves on her plate."

141

Sarah got out of the car and followed the driver's pointing arm across a wide and increasingly fertile expanse of the Judean hills. Far away in the distance, glimmering gold in the sunshine, she could see the Mecca.

"Yerushalayim!" said the man, enthusiastically. "How you say? Jerusalem!"

"He wanted to show us Jerusalem," said Sarah, climbing into the back seat of the car beside Adela. "And it did look golden in the sun. Cheer up, soon we'll be in Jerusalem the Golden. Civilisation. You'll feel much better there."

Adela looked at her sourly. "You believe everything you're told," she said. "How do you know it wasn't Bethlehem?" She turned away from Sarah and gazed, once again, at the barren hills. "Sometimes," she said, "you are not my child at all."

Next morning they walked to the site of the Wailing Wall together, and against her will, the mysterious power which emanated from those hallowed stones awoke a terrible hope in Sarah. There, in the unforgiving sunlight she began to weep, and found that she could not stop. The wall was segregated, cordoned off, like an orthodox synagogue, and on the men's side, behind a rope stood those ancient gnarled and twisted figures in the now familiar dusty garb, their skins, under their prayer shawls, yellowing with age like the pages in the holy books they had spent their lives bent over. Sarah had no sympathy for these relics, fanatical lost souls, praying and keening with such sweaty fervour. She watched through her tears as they wrapped

142

messages on crumpled paper in strands of their own hair and pushed them into cracks between the massive and unyielding stones.

And on her side stood many shapeless women, their heads and arms covered with woven cloth, entirely absorbed in weeping. So much pain, and so much history were here, and somehow it seemed it was Sarah's history, the history of the bereaved. She began to sob in great, racking sobs, and, copying the loathed "fanatics", wrote out a message, pulled out some strands of her hair to wind around it, then thrust it into the nearest crack in the wall. She turned away and found Adela watching her with horror.

"What was that all about?" Adela asked, putting her arm round Sarah's waist and leading her away. And as Sarah continued weeping, Adela gave her a sharp smack on her bottom, as if she were a naughty little girl. "Stop it. Stop it at once. There's to be no more crying, do you hear?"

Gradually, Sarah's sobs died away, and Adela said, "I don't understand. What are they all doing at that Wall? Who are these messages for? Who was your message for? Was it for God, or for Adam?"

"I don't know," gulped Sarah. "I don't know." She blew her nose. "It's silly, isn't it? Do you know what I wrote? I only wrote 'I love you'."

Adela sat her daughter-in-law down at a café table and ordered coffee and honey cakes with cinnamon and fresh cream eclairs.

"Eat a little sweetness," she commanded, patting Sarah's hand. "You are, after all, my child."

9

Sarah lay listening to the noises of the old house and the gentle, insistent sound of rain falling on deep countryside outside. The bedroom was cold with that special coldness of country bedrooms in the early morning light. Rob had read Keats to her last night, before they'd gone to sleep:

> St. Agnes' Eve – Ah, bitter chill it was!
> The owl, for all his feathers, was a-cold,

and she'd got up just before dawn and gone, shivering, to the bathroom, watching the rain fall on stable roofs, on trees, lawn, and distant hills. When she crept back to bed she could not fall asleep again, and daringly, she laid her cold feet on Rob's calves, but he did not stir, lying beside her, warm and sweet, like the child they should have had, his breathing silent and natural as the rainfall.

She had wanted to give it one more chance, but she knew, deeply, it could never work. How could she commit herself entirely to someone she'd sought out as an antidote to pain? Real love took no account of purpose: it must contain that pain, as well as all the sweetness and the light.

She lay beside a man she loved, and who loved her, and whose body had power to comfort her, but she had suffered a loss for which there could be no comfort. The knowledge settled on her, colder than the chilling rain, colder than snow: there could be other seasons, other lovers, but never could there be replacement. What was love for, if it could not save the one you loved?

Bitterly, she cried, in the cold light of early morning, the tears sliding out of the sides of her eyes as she'd discovered they do when one is lying down. Hot and wet, they drenched her temples and her hair, but the centre of her body ached with a frozen ache as if she was actually under a weight of snow. She moved towards Rob, towards the warmth of him. She murmured his name.

"What's-a-matter?" He was still asleep.

"Nothing." She shivered. "I've got the horrors."

He moved her into the crook of his arm. He stroked her hair.

Later, they made love, and now they lay together like a bulb in the dark earth, his thighs folded round hers in a perfect curve, his root inside her core in the perfect dark. Would they ever flower again, as brilliantly as they had just done, in another spring?

Gradually, the noises of the old house reasserted themselves once more above the turmoil in her blood, and the sound of the rain became, again, the only insistent sound. Here it is, she thought, the golden valley, hemmed by blue hills, here it is, the gracious house, set among trees and lawns, empty and waiting. Downstairs, a dog and a cat move about familiarly, there are donkeys in the paddock and a hen or two to lay us speckled brown eggs for breakfast. In a corner room, windowed on two sides, a man and a woman lie in that special ease after love.

His weight was just right for her. Even the place where his ribs had been broken in a school rugger scrum did not press into her today, did not hurt her. Earlier, she had heard the high, wild cry of the Siberian geese who migrated each winter to the golden valley, and knew now that the sound must have come from her own throat. I could lie here for ever, she thought. How I wish we could make it work. Then Rob woke and moved away from her, his skin making a brisk suction sound as he detached his body from their mutual warmth and moistness.

He swung out of bed and kissed her lightly, counting up months on his fingertips. "What sort of baby will that be?" he asked, grinning at her. "Aquarius? Aries? Scorpio?"

She laughed. "None of those," she said. "I'll have to work it out." And the day began.

They knocked on the door of a cottage at the end of a lane in remote, hilly country, but all was dark within, and no one answered. "That's odd," said Rob, his brow puckered. "I thought the old boy's wife was ill. Well, perhaps she's been taken to hospital and he's gone to visit her. We'll come back this way after our walk."

It was a long walk full of marvels, for the light, that sullen, wintry sunshine which comes after rain and is touched with indigo threats at its edges, lit up meadows so they gleamed silver for long moments. Black sheep stood dripping against the wet greenness. Raindrops glittered on bare hedgerows, lichen grew on twisted crab apple trees and there were wands of wet diamonds everywhere. But by far the best marvel to Rob was the noble sight of Guinness, his beloved wolfhound, loping along before them, for Guinness had recently been shot at by a farmer for chasing sheep; had been wounded and was only now showing a return to his usual vigorous form.

"You can see he's well again by the gloss on his coat," said Rob happily. "And that reminds me. Do you know what they were saying about you, in the pub? Oh, we've seen her, they said, she's been in here with her hair all glossy. You can tell she's getting what she needs. You can always tell." Rob looked smug. "Like a good glossy coat on a dog," they said. "She's getting what she wants."

Suddenly Guinness jumped through a gap in a black-thorn hedge after a pregnant ewe lying helpless in a ditch. Rob jumped after him, to restrain him, and together, man and dog startled the terrified ewe back to the flock.

"Well, that's our good deed for the day," said Rob, with satisfaction.

There was a light in the cottage on the way back and the old woman let them in. Her husband had disappeared into the back of the house, which was built right into the hill, and while they were waiting for him, she told them of her first illness in all of her seventy years. She was a strong-looking woman, with handsome bones and sparse white hair swept up with dignity from a fine, clear face, but she described the indignities of pain, of tests inflicted on her by the local hospital. Sarah recognised the tone of outrage in her voice.

Rob, who was pale with cold, and had kept his coat on against the chill tidiness of the tiny front room, went paler still. Sarah looked at him, protectively. His mother had died in the local hospital. His uncle had died

147

of a perforated ulcer. He, Rob, had experienced just such pains. She wanted to tell him he would be all right: she would never let it happen to him. Didn't he know that she loved him, and that love was a spell, a charm more powerful than any magic? I'll never let them get you, she thought, echoing her early morning thoughts.

What was love for, if it could not save the one you loved?

With a shock, she realised that she still believed in Love the great deliverer, and in the power of Love, in spite of everything.

From barium meal tests, the old woman got on to the hospital Christmas pantomime, and from there to the rally drivers who sometimes shattered the peace of their cottage under the hill by having accidents on the bend outside. "There was one boy crashed just recently," she said, "and they brought him in and laid him on the carpet – I had him carried into the kitchen. Well, after all, I couldn't let him stay in here. He was bleeding all over my clean carpet."

There was a creaking on the open wooden staircase and the old man, who had been a schoolteacher of Rob's, joined them, and settled himself in his old chair. He patted a copy of a pamphlet Rob had written on the conservation of a local castle, which was sticking ostentatiously from his pocket. "Something here I'd like you to sign for me. If you would," he said. "I've my criticisms, mind. Grammar, mostly. And punctuation."

He drew the pamphlet from his pocket and they saw that it had been heavily annotated. "I reckon you're big enough, these days, to take it," he admonished Rob, who shrank further and further into his hiking coat. "Mind you," the old man said to Sarah, his voice taking on the pulpit tone of one who quotes himself too often:

148

"I always say I'll buy a book for one good sentence, though, of course I'm not saying there's only one good sentence here."

The old woman brought a tray of weak coffee in blue willow cups and buttered scones of a curious, lumpen texture. "She's supposed to be in bed," her husband grumbled in affectionate tones. "But she still cooks. I told her the other day that what I fancied most were the hot cross buns she makes at Easter. And though it isn't Easter, she made them for me."

He chewed thoughtfully, as his wife went up to bed, and when he had masticated and swallowed the last crumbs he told them about the blackthorn stick, a stout beauty he'd cut and polished for her so she could bang on the bedroom floor if she felt bad, and he'd be bound to hear her. "We've got a code," he explained. "One knock, and she wants a cup of tea. Two, and she's feeling faint and needs my attention, and her medicine. Three knocks and she's settling down to sleep."

"As soon as she's better I'll finish my memoirs," he said. And turning to Sarah, added, "Byron's publishers in London promised to publish them twenty-five years ago. And I wasn't young, then . . . Ah," he said, "there's ambition for you. Sleeping deep as coal. But still there, underground."

Or preserved under glass, like all these carefully polished paperweights, thought Sarah.

Rob had wandered to a bookshelf and taken down Shakespeare's sonnets. "'Bare ruin'd choirs where late the sweet birds sang,'" he read. "Ah, yes, I remember when you read this to us . . . you said it referred to the dissolution of the monasteries. I wonder, were you right?"

"We Celts are obsessed with the subject of Death," the old man said, reprovingly, "ageing and death. But when I was young and went to Paris – "

A loud knocking on the ceiling with the blackthorn stick. Two knocks. The old man looked heavenwards.

"She calls," he said, and clattered slowly up the stairs.

"We must get an onion," Rob was saying, when he came back down. "I can't eat steak without onions."

"I'll give you one," said the teacher. "A homegrown onion. A literary onion. Know your onions." He seemed cheerful, Sarah thought. Perhaps the old woman felt better. He disappeared into the kitchen under the hill, and called out: "Did you want one, or two?"

The sky was fierce with stars and the old man talked of Orion as he gave them his homegrown onions. There was no moon, and despite the starlight, the way ahead was very black.

"Do you have a torch?"

Rob shook his head.

"Shall I lend you one?"

"No need. Our eyes will soon accustom to the darkness."

"'When I lie where shades of darkness
Shall no more assail mine eyes – '

– There he goes again, you'll say," the old man chuckled. "Death is always on his mind. I must go in. She may need me."

He hugged them both farewell, gripped Rob's arm, and was gone, taking the hard-edged triangle of light from the cottage doorway with him.

Rob took Sarah's hand and they walked a little way

in blindness, turning towards each other when their sleeves brushed and stopping to kiss, intently and in passion, a long, affirming kiss. They put a great deal into that kiss: relief at having escaped from a house where only the past lived and death knocked daily on the ceiling with a blackthorn stick; certainty of their future; pride in each other, and at the vigour of their feelings. When they looked up again they could see Guinness streaking along between black hedges, his creamy white coat clearly visible in the starlight.

"Follow my Guinness!" said Rob. "I could have killed you in there when you told me to take my coat off. I've never been so cold."

"I loved you in there," she told him, "you were so funny, so pale and prickly."

"What do you mean?" asked Rob, suspiciously, but he took her hand again, and together they walked forward confidently into the darkness.

A week later Guinness was killed crossing the railway track near the house.

A month later Rob was unfaithful to her.

And that season the Siberian geese with the high, wild cry left the golden valley never to return.

It was not for some time, therefore, that Sarah learned that the lady of the blackthorn stick had died that very night.

10

We'll have Manhattan
The Bronx and Staten
Island too –
It's lovely going through
The Zoo –

The light-hearted lilt of the old song wafted innocence
and uncomplicated happiness Sarah's way as she stood,
drink in hand, staring entranced through endless plate-
glass windows at the cloud-capped towers, the
gorgeous skyscrapers, the solemn temples, the gardens
of glittering, hanging lights in this, the new Babylon.
She raised her glass to the famous skyline in a silent
toast, swaying slightly to the music. The aspirant city
had done it again: she felt carefree, elated, silly. She had
escaped. She felt she could float out and dance across
town as in a musical. For the first time she could remember since Adam died, Sarah was happy in a foolish,
light-hearted kind of way.

"What's New York like?" David had asked her on the
telephone.

"What do you think it's like?"

"Giant skyscrapers crammed with hamburgers on
every floor, and as you go up and up they become
cheeseburgers and then whoppers, you know. And the
whole building ends in a kind of crown at the top made
of milkshakes and chocolate nut sundaes in those tall

knickerbocker glory glasses, so it looks really yummy, up there in the sky."

He's not entirely wrong, she thought, smiling to herself. Then Mel had asked: "Have you fallen in love yet?"

"Only – as usual – with the New York skyline."

"Don't expect that to reassure me. It's got to be the seventh most phallic wonder in the world."

"What are the others?"

"Wouldn't you like to know!"

"Admiring the city?"

A tall, blond, carefully hewn example of East Coast man stood looking down at her, wearing a well-cut smile.

"Drew Andrews," he said, transferring his martini, and holding out a large, square, clean-cut right hand.

"It was quite amazing how much I could tell about Andrew J. Andrews the Third," Sarah was to say, long afterwards. "At that very first meeting, before I knew anything at all."

She knew, for instance, that this man's life was regulated by the seasons, and by the sports that are played in each season, and the apparel appropriate to each season and its sports. She knew that his day was regulated by the time of meals in relation to those sports, that his lunches would be at the Club – the Harvard, or the Yacht, or possibly the N.Y. Athletic Club. She could have sworn he played squash before lunch, and poured his first drink on to rocks at six, then bathed, dressed and went out for an early dinner with friends. The odd thing was, that if she'd encountered so predictable a man in London, she would almost certainly have been bored by him. Here, however, among the electric skyscrapers, she found him reassuring.

"Could I freshen your drink for you?" Such courtesies! The East Coast was the last repository of good manners, just as it was of good, old-fashioned English usage. "What *was* that? A Bloody Mary?"

"It was a Virgin Mary, actually," Sarah told him. "But this time I'll have some vodka in it. Why not live dangerously? We *are* on the thirty-fourth floor!"

"You're English!" he said, delighted. "Actually – " he drawled out the syllables of the absurd word, then laughed, "I did my post-graduate year at Oxford. Saint John's College. Or rather, Sinjuns." He took her glass from her. "Back in a shake. Don't jump, now."

We'll go to Yonkers
Where true love conquers
In the wilds –

He stared at her, when he returned, as if she were something to eat. "Cheers!" he said. "Skol! Your health!"

"Have a nice day!" Sarah said, demurely.

"You're smiling!" he accused her. "Do you know how seldom the corners of women's mouths turn up?"

"I was thinking about my little boy," she said, and told him about the skyscrapers bursting with hamburgers.

"I like it," Drew Andrews said. "Why did you leave him behind? Kids adore New York."

"School," said Sarah. "And I'm working here. I wouldn't have the proper time for him."

"Where's your husband?"

"Dead."

"Oh – I'm sorry."

"No need to be. It's not your fault."

"What's the work?"

"I write features for newsapers and magazines. I'm interviewing people about divorce for a series which keeps getting cancelled, then revived. Do you qualify?"

"Never been married. Engaged twice. Broke it off."

Sarah surveyed him over her brilliantly blended crushed-ice Bloody Mary. "*You* broke it off?" she asked. "Both times?"

He grinned and nodded. "Yeah," he said. "But I haven't given up. Still plan to be a married man some day."

Warning signals went off in Sarah's head but she ignored them, taking a long swallow of her Bloody Mary and turning back, as if mesmerised, to the lights of the venal city.

"The streets down there look like necklaces – strung on the neck of night," she told him. It must be the jet lag. She felt wonderful. "This is the first time in a long while I've been cheerful," she said, confidingly. "I feel as if something marvellous was just about to happen."

Drew Andrews gazed at her solemnly then, for a long moment. "I think it has," he said. "I think it just has." He laughed uneasily. "It's making me nervous. Come on, this party's ending. I'll see you home."

"You won't when you hear where I'm staying. I'm miles uptown in a period mansion on Riverside Drive, with friends. A huge, derelict Jesuit house undergoing conversion, bit by loving bit."

"Try me. I've a limo waiting. Goes with the job."

"Wall Street?"

"You got it. Investment analysis. But I should have been an actor."

155

Sirens wailed loudly in the streets below, or were they more warning signals in her head? To hell with it! There was something wistful about Drew Andrews, at odds with the clean, sporting bulk of him; he wasn't predictable at all, he was a puzzle and she always found puzzles attractive.

He held his hand out to her, she took it, and they left the party like teenagers, together.

> The city's glamour can never spoil
> The dreams of a boy and goil
> We'll turn Manhattan
> Into an Isle of Joy –

"You sure should get plenty of material here, if what you're writing about is divorce," said the heavily made-up hired hostess of a party in a mansion on Long Island. "The place is crammed full of men with pacemakers and twenty-five-year-old third wives. And by the way, if you want to see over this house, feel free. The Boss likes people to see everything, even inside the closets."

Sarah wandered around among gilded mirrors and gilded statues of little eighteenth-century black boys. She sipped Dom Perignon from a champagne goblet made of solid gold, and her ears were out on stalks.

"He was worth fourteen million at the last count," she overheard, "and the sonofabitch only paid for two operations for me in the whole of our married life. That's how much he cared about my body!"

She lingered behind a golden lamp to hear what the two operations had been. "He paid for my womb to be

156

removed and for my teeth to be recapped. My face-lift, you know, the one I had done on my neck and the lids of my eyes, not the other one, I had to pay for that myself. And I gave that man five years of my one and only life!"

Upstairs, the master bedroom was so large the enormous bed seemed moored forlornly there as if it had grown tired of waiting for a suitably grandiloquent act of love. Photos of the host's ex-wives, as sweethearts, brides and little girls, covered the walls, all framed in gilded heart-shaped frames.

"His third wife left him for the decorator. She just ran off, leaving their two young kids."

"You're out of date, my dear. He married the nanny she'd left them with, a Californian girl, but *she's* just found herself, you know. Decided she ought to be a person, have fun with people her own age. Someone's told her Long Island is confining if what you're searching for is personhood."

"Well, everyone's searching for something."

"That's for sure."

In the master bathroom, approached over acres of knee-high carpet, the sunken bath, Roman-style, and just the size for two, had a golden jacuzzi attached and taps in the shape of gold swans with soap dishes to match, complete with what looked suspiciously like gilded soap. A dark golden Greek key motif appeared instead of grime round the rim of the bath and was echoed in the personalised towels and bathrobes draped luxuriously round the room. Just think of the personalised towels you'd have to chuck out each time you changed wives! It didn't bear thinking of. It would be almost worth while finding wives with the same initials.

A fluffy head-rest fixed to one side of the bath with gold plastic adhesive straps added a touch of supermarket stamp-collector fantasy which Sarah much enjoyed.

She wandered to the window and looked out over the verandah below and the heated, floodlit swimming pool below that. Figures in evening dress, or swimming gear, or mixtures of both, lay idly chatting in reclining chairs.

"One of the nannies drowned in this pool. A Vietnamese."

"We never heard anything."

"It was all hushed up."

A Philippino butler appeared and reported that the host was wanted on the telephone, but the host wouldn't take the call.

"I'm having a party. Who is it, anyway?"

It transpired that the caller was the man's first wife.

"Good God! The bitch hasn't called me in years. I won't talk to her. Get rid of her!" he commanded the diminutive butler, waving his bourbon glass. "Tell her I'm out. Tell her I'm dead." He winked at the assembled company. "Tell her any goddamn thing you like." His guests tittered uneasily as the butler exited and their host mused aloud, "I was married six years to that cow and I'm still here. Her second husband killed himself after six weeks. She must want something. The bitch only calls me if she wants."

There were over-laden children's rooms, with everything a child could want in them, but no children sleeping in the beds. And above the flowery drapes of an empty, child's four-poster, one photograph was pointed out: the puddingy issue of that mystic six-year union just described, grinning into Daddy's camera for ever.

There was a great view over Long Island Sound from

the upstairs windows. Covetable yachts lay serenely at anchor in their own exclusive moorings, and small craft bobbed up and down. Suddenly and violently, Sarah wished Adam were there. How they would laugh at all this golden beastliness. Without him, it all seemed merely beastly. If Adam had been there they'd have been playing *Private Lives*.

"Whose yacht is that?"

"The Duke of Westminster's."

"It always is."

They'd laugh and hug each other and Adam would make some crack about the potency of cheap symbols and Sarah would say, "What's wrong with cheap music?" and he'd say, "That's what I meant, you nana, all those clashing cymbals!"

She descended the staircase and went out, through the throng, towards the pool.

"Who's that doll over there in the transparent dress with the blue bikini underneath?" a man was asking of his wife, who was herself dressed mainly in diamonds. The woman threw him a look of pure contempt. "That's your daughter, you dumbskull," she replied.

Sarah passed the heated area round the pool, skirting the chaise-longues and the attempts, both drunk and sober, to waylay her, and crossed a coarse green lawn towards a stone balustrade with a view over the water. The heels of her evening shoes sank into the turf and she shivered, wishing she'd brought her coat, but she reached the balustrade and stood there for a while, wondering if there was a green light, still, at the end of Daisy's dock, wondering if she should get her coat and go and sit in one of the small boats bobbing there, empty and inviting.

"Whose yacht is that?" said a masculine voice behind her.

"The Duke of Westminster's," she answered. "It always is."

She wheeled round sharply but it was not Adam, it was Drew Andrews, taking off his coat.

"Here," he said, draping it round her and doing a button up in front. "It's cold tonight, or hadn't you noticed?"

It was dark blue woven cashmere, caressingly soft and warm. She was falling in love with his clothes, and she'd only seen him twice! He smiled indulgently down at her. "I'll always look after you," he said. "Oh, I'll look after you better than anyone's ever done before."

Such protectiveness! Such unexpected gentleness! Tears pricked Sarah's eyes before she had time to reflect that she had not asked, had not even wanted, to be looked after. This man had the power to make her feel vulnerable – and that was dangerous. And how on earth had he got here? Had he tracked her down, or was he – like Superman before him – in the rescue business?

She never did find out: in the whole of the time she was to spend with Drew, she found out very little about him. And yet he managed to make her feel extraordinarily close to him, as if they had always, must always, belong to one another. The nerve of it: he had pinched her old trick, the time-honoured way to make yourself truly loved: you sussed out the Other's hidden sensitivities, then played on them with amazing solicitude. It rendered the victim both grateful and dependent, for never had anyone tried to please him with so much delicacy and determination: it demonstrated such depths of understanding, the kind that can only come through love.

And you could do it all without revealing much about yourself. A clear case, Sarah reflected, of the biter bit – for the trouble was, it worked.

It was destiny, you see, this kind of headlong fall into romantic love – a life force, a tidal wave – it was useless to resist it. You could tell it was meant by the day, the date, the time, the position of the moon at that exact moment of all the moments in your life. Why else should they have met at all, poised thirty-four feverish floors above Manhattan? No, chance was altogether too unlikely – it had to be ruled out.

He took her everywhere, in the days that followed, theatre, ballet, the latest restaurants, the very best views. He bought her extravagant presents and paid her absurdly extravagant compliments, and after their very first meeting he sent her a single yellow rose. On the second day, two yellow roses arrived and on the third day, three.

"Who is this yucky person?" asked Daisy, the pre-pubescent daughter of her friend Diana, with whom she stayed. "Is he for real?"

The roses continued, and so did impromptu visits, at coffee stage to the lunchtime haunts where Sarah was meeting her friends. And in between meetings, his phone calls had risen to four, five or even six a day. At the end of the first hectic week, Sarah opened the front door of Diana's house to see Drew standing there, almost hidden behind a weight of flowers: seven separate bouquets, each separately gift-wrapped.

"I think you've overdone it," she said.

"I always do," Drew said. "I always do."

★

He let her talk and laugh and cry about Adam without seeming to throw up and she was deeply grateful to him for his patience. He showed an athlete's interest in the physical manifestations of shock. He steered her, one day, to an exhibition of ancient Chinese gardens at the Met, and pointed out to her how the Chinese had always planted trees and flowers in accordance with the principles of yin and yang, and had used their gardens in every kind of weather, to observe the balance of nature, but never to disturb it. He showed her the small pavilions they'd built in which to take tea and admire inclement weather.

"They planted special broad-leaved trees to enhance the plop of raindrops," he explained. And then he made her read the legend inscribed above the entrance to a tranquil winter garden, and she knew why he had brought her here.

"In China," it said, "the cycle of life and death is profoundly venerated, as are the seasons which reflect it. Garden flowers are not removed as unsightly when they fall, or fade, and die, but are left in the borders as natural contrast to growing things so they can be appreciated as reminders of nature's rhythms. For without the steady contemplation of natural rhythms, how can we hope to inspire in ourselves a harmonious adjustment to nature's forces?"

"I've never seen you like this," Diana said, over coffee and orange juice in the basement kitchen of the derelict mansion where half of a freezing cold flagstone floor had just been uncovered. "You're positively radiant." She went to the door to make sure that Daisy was not in earshot, then added: "He must be marvellous in the sack!"

"I wouldn't know. He hasn't invited me to bed. Do you think I should be flattered, or insulted?"

Diana assumed a knowing expression which failed to conceal a degree of satisfaction. "I knew there was something! A man can't be that perfect. Not nowadays, in a city where almost everyone is three times divorced, or gay."

"What's wrong with old-fashioned courtship?" Sarah asked.

"How should I know? I've never been exposed."

Drew's house was on an islet in Connecticut, a small promontory, so that it had a wooded headland and a small bay entirely to itself. The woodland had been cleared to make lawns around the house and they walked through slim-trunked silver birches and knotty pines to the water's edge, and then along sandy beach.

"We'll make love in the boat, in the summer. And in the hammock, slung between trees, and on the verandah, on my creaky old wicker swing chair. We'll make love right here, where the pine needles fall on sand – "

"They'll stick in me in unmentionable places."

"They won't. I'll spread out my cloak for you, my very best Brooks Brothers cloak. And in winter we'll have a great wood fire in the bedroom and we'll make love in the firelight under my old New England quilt, and you'll come and come and you'll plead with me to stop, and you'll never want to sleep with anyone else, ever again."

They rounded the corner of the bay and stepped out on to a long flat stretch of beach, where there was only sea and sand and sky, and the wind whipping at their faces. They unlinked their arms and moved separately into the wind, as if needing to affirm their separate presences in all this vastness. Sarah's eyes watered, and through the blur she saw the sea coast of America, stretching for thousands upon thousands of miles, inlets and islets and wooded coves, rocks and promontories and deserted beaches, boats hidden in the rushes, and white timbered houses with verandahs and rocking chairs. She could see it all unfold, her new life, for what was America but the New World and the promise of a brand new life? She had been at sea for so long, and she'd been shipwrecked on a wild, barbaric shore.

What country, friends, is this?
This is Illyria, lady.

She had lost her brother, her twin, and she looked for him everywhere, but she found only this oddball Duke, a stranger she would come to love.

Drew stopped some way ahead of her and waited for her to catch up, his arms held wide to reach and hold and hug her, then he put some headphones attached to a tiny black box tenderly to her ears. At once, the long, windy beach was filled with magnificent sounds: the swell of a whole orchestra, a magical piano – the slow movement, Mozart's piano concerto number 21. The oddball Duke must be Orsino, after all. But was he, as Daisy asked, for real?

164

How dost thou like this tune?
It gives a very echo to the seat
where love is throned.

"David would love it here, wouldn't he?" Drew
asked anxiously, as they turned their back on the wind
and made for home. "The swimming, and the boats,
and the picnics in the summer, and the barbecues. And
in winter we'll all go skiing – I'll teach him to ski. Do
you think he'd like that?" He wanted to build a bunk
bed for David, and make a playroom in the loft. He
wanted to make a wigwam for him – there were Indian
ruins (they looked like ordinary granite rocks to Sarah)
in the garden. "Perhaps I should come back with you to
London and meet him there?"

"No. I think it would be more of a knockout for him
to come here and meet you and see all this."

"I'll have my compact car insured for you to drive by
the time you get back," he said. "But I think I'll get you
a little English sports car."

"I haven't learned to drive."

He stared at her in amazement. "Then I'll have to
teach you. You can't live out here without a car."

Oh, the relief she felt at having the practical matters
of life taken out of her hands. Things would be organ-
ised for her, problems would be shared, David would
have a father figure. And Drew was so *presentable*, the
kind of man people expected her to marry. Everyone
would be so pleased, she'd be off their consciences, they
wouldn't have to worry about her anymore. She couldn't
think of a single friend she'd shrink from introducing
Drew to. They'd make a great couple and have a wonderful life. *She'd be part of something.*

165

Drew stopped in a sheltered cove and selected a handful of flat, oval pebbles from the shingly sand.

"This tree trunk, here," he pointed out, "the one with the hollow in it at the level of your waist. A thrush nests here, each year. She lays a nestful of eggs with sky blue shells, maybe five or six of the little beauties. She guards them frantically, of course, but she's lucky if one or two, in any batch, are hatched."

He chose a flat-sided pebble, gripped it between his thumb and forefinger and skimmed it, with careful expertise, across the bay. The stone touched water twice, with satisfying plops, throwing up ducks and drakes and ever widening circles.

"I think you ought to know, there's never been anything like this," said Drew. "I've never brought anyone here." The ripples fanned and shimmered out as Sarah waited for further information. "I shared an apartment with one, for quite a while. With the other, I regret to say, I just moved in on her."

"What happened in the end?"

Drew skimmed another stone, and watched it hit the water.

"I just cleared out," he said. "It was the only thing to do."

Sarah stared at him, unperturbed. How could such revelations touch or threaten her? She was here, among thrushes' nests and ducks and drakes, enshrined at the heart of the fairy tale. She'd only ever liked the ones that had happy endings.

And so they continued to match their fantasies, each to each: they'd have a house in France each summer; they'd motor through Tuscany each winter; they'd honeymoon in Venice, where neither of them had ever been. Easter would traditionally be reserved for Paris and that special little Left Bank hotel, but Christmas would be in snowy Connecticut, in front of big wood fires, or under antique quilts. She would keep her London flat, of course, and maybe rent it some of the time, to academics.

And Drew had been negotiating for some months past to buy a bunch of women's magazines. He'd always fancied himself as a print tycoon or newspaper proprietor. Sarah could have her own magazine to run, if that was what she wanted. At the very least, she'd have receptive markets for her work.

She watched the play of fantasies as if they were fireworks on 4th July, exploding way off across Bar Harbour and seen only dimly from down the coast of Maine, but though she thought she was watching out, bits of reality got mixed into their dreams until neither of them could tell which was which.

Beautifully dressed – Drew had bought her a black velvet cloak lined with ivory satin – Sarah waited in the foyer of the Opera House for Drew to show up. Elegant people in evening dress greeted each other, then pushed past her into the auditorium. It was getting late, and she wondered a little, because Drew had always been first to get to their meeting places.

Should she go in, and leave his ticket at the box office? She couldn't do that, because Drew had the tickets. Naturally. The foyer emptied and she was left, standing almost alone, fielding the curious glances of commissionaires. The strains of the overture – it was

Don Giovanni – could be heard through the thickly padded doors. She sat down on the stairs. She wandered about. She went outside and stood on the steps and looked up and down the street. No Drew.

After an hour or so, she went home to the dark mansion at Riverside Drive and let herself in. There was no one at home, and the huge, empty house echoed her footsteps as she stepped over holes in the floorboards, and rescued the hem of her velvet cloak from the builders' dust which lay over everything.

She took a tray with a glass of milk and a sandwich up to her spacious room, undressed and got into the great carved bed. Diana had left the latest funny books by her bedside, but she couldn't read; there were no curtains, yet, at the big windows that overlooked the Hudson River, and she watched the branches of the tall, potted trees Diana had temporarily housed in her room, making patterns on the walls.

This place was like the sleeping beauty's castle, lying almost invisible under dusty cobwebs, waiting to be reawakened into the modern world. But the prince who was to administer the kiss of life had disappeared. If he never turned up again, would she be trapped, for ever, in the past? And what am I doing here, like an idiot, waiting for a prince's kiss, she wondered, lying back against the Edwardian lace-edged pillows. Aren't I supposed to have my own real life? I want to be independent but I'm always getting waylaid, in my quest, by love. The truth is, I want both love and independence, and it seems they are incompatible.

Suddenly, the bell clanged, echoing through the house, an ancient, gong-like sound. Ah, Drew! At last! She jumped out of bed and put on a robe, then made her way cautiously downstairs, through dustsheets that lay, like perilous shrouds, over the dark and cavernous stairwell. She must make sure it was him, of course. It could be burglars, or muggers or rapists. This was, after all, New York. They'd never forgive her if she opened the door to strangers in the night.

She peered through the heavy frosted glass and wrought-iron grill of the door and saw three outlines standing there, laughing and digging one another in the ribs. Young hooligans! Had they seen her? Would they try to break down the door? The clang of the bell resounded once more about the house. Sarah waited until it had died away, then climbed the three flights, despondently, to her room. What had happened to Drew? Had he been in an accident? Was he lying somewhere, hurt? Could he have been mugged or killed?

The telephone rang, and she picked up the receiver by her bed.

"Oh, Sarah," said Daisy's teenage voice. "It's you. Could you possibly let me in? I've forgotten my keys."

"Was that you and your mates at the door?"

"Yes, it was. I'm really sorry to disturb you."

"You think he's dumped me, don't you?" Sarah accused Diana next morning, over the breakfast tray her friend had brought her. "You think he was scared."

"They're all scared," Diana said. "The moment they get close to a female human being, it's Mommy all over again and they have to run for their lives. Cutting loose – that's what it means to be a man."

"The drive away from the mother," Sarah muttered to herself.

"What's that?"

"Oh, nothing. You don't seem to realise, I'm worried witless. I think of him lying in a morgue somewhere. Or under the wheels of a car . . ."

"Resign yourself, Sarah. He left. I called every hospital in town last night, as well as his house in Connecticut. You know I did, you were breathing down my neck. This morning we'll call all the office numbers we can find. But I told you, I know these types. He's a bolter, like that Nancy Mitford character. Too good to be true. There had to be something."

"The Bolter was a woman," Sarah reminded her. "Let's give him half a chance."

"What was so great about him, anyway?" Daisy asked, entering the room and helping herself to orange juice. "You two amaze me, you really do, the way you behave over men. I mean, look at the way Mum always kowtows to Dad, as if he was some kind of god."

"The king of the castle," Diana said, amused.

"The prince in the fairy tale," echoed Sarah.

"Ugh. Fairy tales!" Daisy gave an exaggerated shudder. "I bet you haven't read any soppy crap like that for years. The women always had a rotten time, and they never *did* anything, as far as I can see. They lived 'happily ever after', it always says, but they might as well have been dead once they'd married the stupid prince."

"Happily ever after," Diana echoed. "She's right, you know. It sounds like a prayer for the dead."

★

Diana got through, two days later, to someone in Drew's office who mentioned a conference in Switzerland.

"So that's his whereabouts. And no one but you seems in the least concerned about his welfare," she said briskly. "I ran into someone at lunch who told me he's been talking of buying that magazine group for years. He hasn't got anything like the bread a deal like that would take. It's a pipe-dream, like everything else."

"I have to give him the benefit of the doubt," said Sarah.

"He doesn't deserve it," Diana chided.

But Sarah had given him several days' chance, all the same, and now she was forced to admit he had run out on her, abandoned her, disappeared.

You chickened out, you stood me up, you let me down, she ranted to herself, striding across Central Park, weeping into the wind. If you'd got in too deep, you could have told me. You could have trusted me. I'd have understood. We would have broken the dream together, Drew. I'm grieving for you, she told him, silently. For everything we had, however brief. For everything we could have had. For there was something real, amid all that fantasy, if only the sheer human comfort of your bulk. I want your arms around me. You were someone to lean on, Drew. I want to hold you when you cry and I want you to hold me when I cry. More than anything, I want that.

The wind from the open sea blew through the canyons of the city on to that blasted heath and froze the tears on Sarah's lashes, while the lights in the sky-scrapers glittered heartlessly. I'm grieving for what we had, for the whole damn fairy tale. What weak, foolish creatures we women are, with our surface cynicism, our fake realism about the world, our brave talk about independence. I don't believe in fairy tales. I'm reasonably grown up. Yet the first prince that offers me that corny happy ending, I turn round and grasp it, with both hands.

"We grasp the fairy tale!" she shouted into the wind, as she turned down Fifth Avenue. "We are fools! Fools!" She wiped her eyes and nose and strode on fiercely past the religions and philosophies of the world, past the hot pretzels and cold orange juice and the lighted windows offering seasonal myths. I don't want to be *part of anything*, she muttered. What an idiot I am. I want to be me, myself. What did Mel say? It's not easier to live through other people. It is necessary to be oneself. Not merely necessary, but right!

Marriage! Husbands and wives as people to lean on. That isn't Love, it's mere dependency. One has to stand tall by oneself. "One person has a life and the other shares it," Sarah had been fond of saying of the state of marriage, when she herself was a very young wife, so many years ago. One couldn't, one mustn't, tolerate a half life.

She crossed the road with the crowd on "Walk" and made for Park Avenue. One thing about this town: there were so many crazies on the streets that one more female talking to herself attracted nobody's attention.

"This wouldn't have happened if you hadn't died," she yelled out loud at Adam. She tripped and almost fell over something which stuck out at an angle on the sidewalk.

"Watch where you're going," said a rich, plummy female voice. "And pick up my book, if you don't mind."

She had fallen over a leg, and the leg, which was well wrapped up in layers of scarves and leg warmers of different colours, a veritable Mother Courage of a leg, belonged to a bag lady, sitting by a brazier, in the corner doorway of one of New York's monoliths. Sarah picked up the book. It was a paperback edition of Sartre's play *Huis Clos*.

"Ah. Hell is other people," she said, automatically, handing it to the woman and seeing a nut-brown face, dwarfed by a moth-eaten fur hat, and lively hazel eyes which looked at her shrewdly and with candour.

"*What* wouldn't have happened if *who* hadn't died?" the woman asked, without removing her stare from Sarah's face. "Here, sit on this step and have a Polo. The mint with the hole. A graphic character portrait of a lot of men I've known." The bag lady shook with laughter, removed a few of her bags and bundles, and patted the cold stone step invitingly, as if it were a club armchair. Bags from Saks and Bendels and Bloomingdale's predominated: you meet a better class of bag lady on Park.

Sarah sat down and told the woman briefly what had happened. She thought it sounded quite impressive: husband dead, lover – or potential lover – gone.

"Fuck that," said the bag lady, tartly. "You don't need it. I had all that myself. I had it twice. Never give it a thought, these days, I promise you."

Her eyes looked away from Sarah, down the Avenue, and they danced with memories.

173

"I had the house on the water, and the verandah and the rocking chair; I had the husband in insurance, and the statutory child, though I didn't like her much when she grew up. I had plenty of good acting parts in the theatre, even if it was only summer stock. But my husband had to have open heart surgery, a triple by-pass, and they didn't know how to do it so well back in those days. It's a long time ago.

"Well, he died. He didn't give himself, or them, a chance. He was smoking non-stop in the hospital with all the tubes still sticking out of him. It was a disgrace. The nurses smuggled the cigarettes in for him, I suppose. He charmed them with his jokes. And then, after he died, I fell in love. The real thing, you know, the fairy tale. And then *he* died of cancer. I nursed him, but there was nothing I, or anyone, could do."

The bag lady fished in a pocket and brought out a tattered photograph: a man with a splendid physique up what looked suspiciously like a gum tree in some summer place. He wore only shorts and a panama hat and he grinned engagingly. He was brown and had clearly been swimming. The sun shone. Sarah looked from the woman on the sidewalk to the sunburned figure in the snap.

"Why didn't you go on acting?" she enquired.

"Oh, I gave up everything, then," the bag lady said. She stared at the photograph and Sarah continued to stare at her.

"Something in me died, when he died," the woman said. She dragged her gaze from the snapshot to glance at Sarah and there was a disturbing smugness in her face. "Yes," she repeated, smugly. "Something in me died."

174

Something clicked then in Sarah, and she felt it physically, as if her womb and her heart and lungs and the major organs in her body were being rearranged; doors opened and shut inside her and she thought: No. I won't let that happen to me.

She stood up and looked down at the bag lady. She owed it to Adam not to let even a part of her die. She owed it to Adam to live for both of them. She had been left alive, and she had to learn to be alive, and to be herself, alive. She owed it to herself.

"I have to go," she said. "I'm catching a plane to London tomorrow. It's been really good to talk with you."

"It's been pleasant meeting you," the bag lady said, wistfully. And then, remembering her role, she rallied, took a swig from a medicine bottle and started singing: "I care for nobody, no not I, and nobody cares for me. Can I offer you a slug?"

"You're very generous. But, no. You keep it."

"I don't need it, you know," the bag lady said defiantly. "I don't need anything."

The aeroplane gained height, and one by one, the green lights at the end of private docks grew smaller and the arms of tiny harbours fell, beseeching still, away. The lights in the tallest spires of the urban fairy tale glittered, but dwindled, and at every thousand feet the airship climbed, Sarah felt lighter. Hopes, dreams, dependencies, fell away from her like fevers: she almost expected to see them fall, like the bag lady's bundles, into the distant sea. At last, she was floating free, and as

175

the plane levelled out at thirty thousand feet, and hung, apparently motionless, in the sky, she felt that she'd shed all past, and pictured no future, she was simply who she was, now, at this moment in space. Alone.

Something in me died.

The bag lady's words echoed in her head, and once again Sarah's whole being rejected them. She was truly alive, she was here and now, she was alone with her own resourceful self inside the fragile capsule of her body. There was a hum in the pressurised air, a real pooh of a hum, as David would say. She was going home to David, to London, to an unimagined future full of changes she could not foresee. Well, she would meet them when they came.

The plane sped on, a vast mechanical whale travelling the skies, as unlikely a proposition as the human self, complex, fragile, unique, describing its improbable arc between death and life.